DATE

the EISENHOWER ERA

the EISENHOWER ERA

The Age of Consensus

Paul S. Holbo
University of Oregon

Robert W. Sellen
Georgia State University

The Dryden Press
901 North Elm Street
Hinsdale, Illinois 60521

To Kay and Donna
and
Our Not So Silent College Classmates of the 1950's

Cover Credit:
U.P.I. Compix

Contents

the EISENHOWER ERA

Introduction

Every era has many faces but often only a single name. The Americans who reached maturity in the years after the Second World War became known at the time as "the Silent Generation," a label now apparently fixed. The implication is that younger persons in the 1950's, college students in particular, were apathetic, materialistic, and apolitical conformists concerned chiefly for their personal security. Contemporary liberal intellectuals complained further that these attitudes reflected the dominant values of the society as a whole and especially of corporation executives. The characteristic image in this view of the 1950's was that of the Madison Avenue "organization man" dressed in a gray flannel suit.

All that the era offered politically—according to the same critics and other cynical or partisan observers—was Dwight David Eisenhower, typically with a golf club in his hand and a broad but vapid grin on his face. After a brief flirtation with the General before the election of 1952, the liberal intellectuals compared him unfavorably with their standard for president, Franklin D. Roosevelt. They gave

"Ike" especially low marks for his seeming aloofness from politics, his refusal to battle publicly with Senator Joseph McCarthy, and his reluctance to assume active party leadership. As the 1950's wore on, these critics complained that the President failed both to enforce aggressively the Supreme Court's ruling against segregated schools and to lead in the battle for Negro rights, that he was unduly impressed by wealthy businessmen and overly concerned for a balanced budget, and that he had reduced military expenditures to the point of endangering the nation's security. In 1960 the young Democratic candidate for President, John F. Kennedy, echoed this indictment as he campaigned successfully on the theme that it was time to "get this country moving again."

Like all extreme views, these interpretations of Americans in the 1950's and of the Eisenhower administration are partly caricatures. The 1950's were in fact a time of diversity. Witness the growing bohemian set, the advent of abstract expressionism in art, the beatniks and bop music in popular culture, the drive for civil rights (which quickly captured support especially among the young), and a phalanx of conservative intellectuals. There was intense if not always overt political feeling, particularly over issues of foreign policy. Even the supposedly apathetic college students had convictions, or at least instinctual responses, to international issues. They remembered their fathers, brothers, and neighbors going off to war, or had themselves already been in the service, and they *knew* that isolation was impossible and the neglect of military defence criminally foolish. These were profoundly held ax ioms, with which few students openly disagreed and which their teachers and professors accepted or ardently espoused.

There was almost no opposition on college campuses to the involvement of the United States in the Korean War, and only scattered objection to the strategy of limited conflict. Any protesters would have found themselves ostracized by fellow students and by professors alike. Some college officials took advantage of the war to eliminate troublesome extracurricular activities on the ground that it was improper for students to behave frivolously while others were dying for their country and for the United Nations. The president of Yale University in 1951 put an end to the rowdy annual beer-drinking party called "Derby Day" that had for years accompanied crew races on the nearby Housatonic River, and the students somewhat reluctantly bowed to his decision. Within months many of these clean-cut young men exchanged their button-down collars, Repp ties, and natty blazers for the garments of war. Some even went willingly. A few, of course, headed for graduate or professional school with special deferments—the scholarly advance party for the draft-escapers of a generation later, but in the beginning insignificant in number and importance.

To point out the fallacies of the stereotypes of an era is a useful point of departure but does not get one very far. A more interesting frame of reference for this decade is provided by journalists, intellectuals and scholars as they responded to the new post-war climate of prosperity and national confidence. Their efforts to describe current social and political trends, to account for them, and to explain their presumed significance were among the important phenomena of the decade. The theories of social and political behavior or of the *unique* American character that they devised, which gave rise to the so-called "consensus" interpretations, are a major subject of this book.

The consensus intellectuals of the 1950's can more easily be understood by first recalling the dominant views of the 1930's. Economic problems resulting from the Great Depression stimulated "progressive" ideas about the conflict between social classes or between labor and capital through all eras of American history. These ideas lost favor during the Second World War, when the emphasis was placed upon unity in the grim struggle against the Axis powers. After victory became a reality, many intellectuals found the old progressive ideas about domestic divisions and economic problems to be uncomfortable or not to fit the times. They came up with new explanations, to which critics gave the name "consensus," stressing the prosperity, progress, substance, and comparative harmony of American life.

Consensus thought suited an era when the United States was by far the most powerful and prosperous nation in the world. It must be emphasized, however, that consensus ideas such as the pervasiveness of prosperity were dramatically new and striking at that time. Many Americans who remembered vividly the depression of the 1930's feared that it would return, while others were beginning to enjoy the new plenitude but did not quite comprehend the accompanying mores of social adjustment and the politics of moderation.

Consensus interpretations originally played down the importance of liberal ideology in American life, but themselves provided a kind of philosophy for the 1950's. An understanding of consensus thought is crucial to an appreciation of the general mind of the Eisenhower Era, of the leading ideas of the time, and of negative reactions to such views at the time and subsequently—both by academics and those of the New Left. What, then, were the values that gave rise to consensus thought? In what forms was consensus thought expressed? What was the meaning of consensus?

The first section of this volume consists of selections from writings of the 1950's that can help us to answer these questions. The first excerpt, from Sloan Wilson's popular novel, *The Man in the Gray Flannel Suit*, is particularly suggestive for its depiction of a rising young organization man of the post-war period. The hero of the volume, however, is a decent man and does not fulfill the stereotype that the book's title inspired.

Russell Lynes, Jr., describes the goals and values of family men and college students of the period. The passages from his book may be read along with those by fellow journalist Frederick Lewis Allen as shrewd and witty informal histories of the decade; but particular attention should be paid to the author's general perspectives. Lynes, like other contemporary social observers, expresses certain reservations about the new ideal of "well-roundedness" even as he records its dominance. Allen, who has a larger point to make, was bent on affirming that the transformation of the economy and society fully justified confidence in the future of the American system. This assumption is a key feature of consensus thought.

Academic historian David M. Potter draws still broader conclusions. His influential book, *People of Plenty*, is less a description of the decade than a volume that reveals the ideas of the 1950's. Potter holds that prosperity (not depression) typifies the American experience, and he considers the condition of plenty so pervasive that he tries to analyze the impact of mobility and economic opportunity on the American character. His theme of prosperity and uniqueness is of the essence of the consensus view.

Two selections follow from the writings of David Riesman, one interpreting the new social pattern of "other-directedness," and a second treating attitudes toward work and the enlightened nature of modern corporate enterprise. Riesman's analysis was extremely influential, and likewise contributed to the development of the consensus perspective. Sociologist Daniel Bell, meanwhile, proclaims the "end of ideology" and the importance of pluralism, adjustment, and compromise in American politics.

Excerpts from the writings of another sociologist, the "progressive" C. Wright Mills, and from a "conservative" historian-philosopher, Russel Kirk, provide marked contrasts to the consensus interpretations. Professor Mills was a scathing critic of what he considered the heartless oppression of the white-collar class by the capitalist system; he was widely read but less influential in the 1950's than a decade later, when the New Left adopted some of his views. Professor Kirk, who addresses deeper issues of political philosophy such as the nature of power, was a reflective, articulate intellectual spokesman for conservatism, which enjoyed a certain rebirth of interest. Yet, it was consensus thought—not conservatism—that dominated the Eisenhower Era.

Economic progress and full employment during the 1950's helped make possible greater opportunity for Black Americans, as Frederick Lewis Allen suggested. There were other forces for change in racial conditions as well. The Reverend Martin Luther King, Jr., eloquent spokesman for Southern Negroes, makes clear in his simple but moving narrative—the Montgomery, Alabama, bus boycott—that the aspirations of his people originated in the search for human dignity and profound Christian faith.

There is a clear relationship between the ideas and the context of the Eisenhower Era and the trends in literature, the arts and education that are brought out in the third section of this book, entitled "Other Directions." Historian Carl Degler argues effectively that writers turned in an age of prosperity from the emphasis of the 1930's on naturalistic depiction of economic hardship and social injustice to the individual's search for identity in an age of conformity, and that architecture and the visual arts likewise revealed the impact of affluence. There was also a lively concern with the public schools in the Eisenhower Era, which led to attacks on the old dogmas of "progressive education" and to new stress on subject disciplines and the quality of instruction, as the writing of Arthur Bestor reveals. Educational excellence, too, was possible only in an age of prosperity, which permitted such new directions.

Still other important concerns of the Eisenhower Era, such as the vogue of "realism" in thinking about foreign policy, have been omitted for lack of space. Suggestions for reading on all these topics appear in the bibliographical essay.

Politics and foreign affairs receive extended attention in the sections dealing with the Eisenhower administration. President Eisenhower had been the victorious commanding general of the Allied armies in Europe during the Second World War and had served as commander of the North Atlantic Treaty Organization (NATO) at the outset of the decade. He was a professional soldier and living symbol of the coming-of-age of the United States in international affairs, but he had avoided the imperial style of another Republican general, Douglas MacArthur. To Americans, he was "Ike," the GI's general as well as the man who had dealt with President Roosevelt, Prime Minister Winston Churchill, and Soviet Marshal Josef Stalin. In 1952 Republican candidate Eisenhower predictably won an overwhelming victory over his Democratic opponent, with more than 34 million votes to Adlai Stevenson's 27.3 million, and he increased his margin in 1956 with 35.6 million to Stevenson's 26 million.

One of the most popular of American presidents during his term, except with most liberal intellectuals, Eisenhower in the mind of the average citizen was a man of integrity and humane instincts who presided calmly and with firmness over a united nation. In the early 1960's, however, he seemed to suffer by comparison with the glamorous, active, strong-handed Democratic chief executives who succeeded him. The selection by Emmet John Hughes, an Eisenhower speech writer who hoped for more dramatic leadership and greater action from John F. Kennedy, exemplifies this view. Former Department of State official Louis J. Halle similarly criticizes what he considers slogans without substance in the Eisenhower-Dulles foreign policies. These attacks may usefully be compared with Eisenhower's actual performance in press conferences and speeches, Dulles's explanation of the administration's principles in foreign affairs, and the contemporary sympathetic account by journalists Roscoe Drummond and Gaston Coblentz of the important Suez Crisis of 1956.

During the late 1960's, the nation grew weary of riots in the cities and turmoil on college campuses, an indecisive and apparently interminable war in Vietnam, soaring inflation, political divisions, and widespread distrust of the national leadership. The 1950's came to seem an attractive era of substance and repose, especially as the lapse of time and passing events cloud memories.

Attitudes toward Eisenhower shifted accordingly. Today he once more enjoys a high reputation, even among some of his former detractors. Garry Wills' account of Eisenhower's shrewdness is a case in point. Other liberals recall approvingly his persistent attempts to limit defense appropriations, his restraint in exercising executive power and sense of Congress's role, and—following the publication of the "Pentagon Papers"—his obvious caution about becoming involved in Vietnam, which contrasts sharply with Theodore Draper's earlier interpretation. Even radicals quote with favor his reference in a parting presidential address to the need for vigilance toward a "military-industrial complex." The original text of this address is included in the readings because of its broad appeal and enduring importance. No one invokes more effectively the wisdom of Eisenhower than his former vice president, President Richard M. Nixon, and Republican advocates of the "New American Majority."

The readings on the Eisenhower administration mirror the changing views of the 1950's. There doubtless will be shifts of opinion again about the record of Republican rule, as about the decade's economic, social, and intellectual history. Scholarly inquiry into these subjects has only begun. But the time for broad reflection is already upon us, and there are ample materials to undertake the task.

The Clash of Views:
Reflections on the 1950's

Was it an era of conformity, selfish concerns, and apathy?

"It was the time of the hula hoop and 'ding-dong school.' Its balladeer was Elvis Presley. . . .
Happiness was owning a car with the new cow-hip fenders, which quickly evolved into tail fins as the decade progressed. . . .
If you were an intellectual, you worried about college students and complained that they did nothing but work and keep their mouths shut. The 'silent generation' you called them, and feared for the future.
The Eisenhower era was not a binge, as the twenties are said to have been. They were the hour of letdown. The country seemed . . . to be embarked instead on a long, leisurely vacation of self-indulgence more appropriate to the middle-aged.
From time to time . . . there was Adlai Stevenson . . . calling us to duty. And there was John Foster Dulles sermonizing us about 'waging peace,' but the truth is that they were about as welcome as an encyclopedia salesman at the cocktail hour."
Russell Baker, "Observer: A Pause to Look Back,"
The New York Times, March 30, 1969.

"When a fellow gets his draft notice in February and keeps on working and planning till June, instead of boozing up every night and having a succession of farewell parties, he has made a very difficult, positive decision. Most make that decision today."

A student at Harvard during the Korean War,
quoted in "The Younger Generation," *Time*,
Vol. 58 (November 5, 1951), 45-52.

"We live in a heavy, humorless, sanctimonious, stultifying atmosphere, singularly lacking in the self-mockery that is self-criticism. Probably the climate of the late 1950's is the dullest and dreariest in all the history of the United States."

Professor Eric F. Goldman, Princeton University,
final lecture to History 307, Modern America,
in the spring of 1959, published as
"Why Doesn't Johnny Laugh?" *University* (Fall 1959), 9.

"When the time comes, it may not be easy, despite the rebirth of Richard Nixon and Elvis Presley, to muster nostalgia for the Fifties. (Davy Crockett and Roy Cohn, Grace Kelly and the Playboy Bunny, My Fair Lady *and adult Westerns, filter tips and instant coffee, Zen and the art of the Roller Derby, Ban the Bomb and togetherness, Harry Belafonte, Jack Kerouac, Dr. Kinsey, and The Golden Age of Television.)*

But some of the words we used to use already have the power to charm, so great is the distance between then and now. . . . Euphemists offered: the Police Action, peaceful coexistence, nuclear blackmail, freedom fighter, . . . desegregation, payola, cleavage, recession, pinko. . . . Irony, ambiguity, complexity were academic passwords that sophomores enacted as apathy. The common language was designed to not say what was meant. . . .

In the fifties, it was dangerous to take anyone at face value. (Are you for real?) In conformist times, you worried about Image (status), doubly anxious because words functioned as costume: are you hip?

Now you're talking (speaking my language). Certain key terms, dig, became juvenile gestures: L7 equalled square (cube or octagon meant supersquare). The three-ring sign meant cool. . . . in, out; with it, from squaresville. Hepcat. Beat/Jazz contributed: daddy-o, pad, bread, gig, slip me some skin. And all that, like, well, you know, man, incoherence. (Holden Caulfield, Marty, Brando and the Method, action painting, the silent generation, Nichols and May, taking the fifth.)

Don't hand me any of that jazz. Take five.

Alienation was the absurd egghead bit. . . . Yes, above all, anti-frantic. Stay cool. Hang loose. No sweat . . . Made in the shade. Big deal . . ."

Howard Junker, "As They Used to Say in the 1950's,"
Esquire, 72 (August 1969), 70-71, 141.

What did "consensus" mean, and was it the essence of the American experience?

"A pretty good rule-of-thumb for us in the United States is that our national well-being is in inverse proportion to the sharpness and extent of the theoretical differences between our political parties. . . . Our history has fitted us, even against our will, to understand the meaning of conservatism. We have become the exemplars of the continuity of history and of the fruits which come from cultivating institutions suited to a time and place, in continuity with the past."

Daniel Boorstin, *The Genius of American Politics*
(University of Chicago, 1953), pp. 3,6.

"The fierceness of the political struggles has often been misleading; for the range of vision embraced by the primary contestants in the major parties has always been bounded by the horizons of property and enterprise. . . . The sanctity of private property, the right of the individual to dispose of and invest it, the value of opportunity, and the natural evolution of self-interest and self-assertion, within broad legal limits, into a beneficent social order have been staple tenets of the central faith in American political ideologies; these conceptions have been shared in large part by men as diverse as Jefferson, Jackson, Lincoln, Cleveland, Bryan, Wilson, and Hoover."

Richard Hofstadter,
The American Political Tradition and the Men Who Made It
(Knopf, 1948), pp. viii.

"The emphasis on consensus and continuity has softened the outlines and flattened the crises of American history. A certain tameness and amiability have crept into our view of things. . . . The conservative frame of reference is giving us a bland history, in which conflict is muted, in which the classic issues of social justice are underplayed, in which the elements of spontaneity, effervescence, and violence in American life get little sympathy or attention. Now that the progressive impulse is subsidiary, scholarship is threatened with a moral vacuum."

John Higham, "Beyond Consensus:
The Historian as Moral Critic," *The American Historical Review*,
LXVII (April 1962), p. 616.

What was the nature of the Eisenhower leadership?

"There is an American Consensus on the issues, but it was developed by Franklin Roosevelt and developed further in some respects by Truman. Eisenhower has been content to leave it undisturbed. . . . Eisenhower did disturb the old political balance of power as distinguished from the consensus on issues, but he had not the energies, the talents, nor the experience to exploit his personal triumphs for his party's advantage. . . . Eisenhower and his administration have lived off the accumulated

wisdom, the accumulated prestige, and the accumulated military strength of his predecessors, who conducted more daring and more creative regimes. If our margin for error is as great as it has traditionally been, these quiet Eisenhower years will have been only a pleasant idyll, an inexpensive interlude in a grim century. If our margin for error is much thinner than formerly, Eisenhower may join the ranks of history's fatal good men . . . [who] bequeathed to their successors a black heritage of time lost and opportunities wasted."

William Shannon, "Eisenhower as President,
Commentary, Vol. 26 (November 1958), p. 398.

"Eisenhower: His reputation is faring remarkably well. It is the reputation of a limited man who carried on a line-and-staff operation and delegated most work to others but who knew his mind and in the end kept from making the war blunders his successors made . . . he vetoed the apocalypse whenever it was proposed."

Max Lerner, "The Big Mangling Machine,"
Chicago Sun-Times, June 26, 1971.

Part One THE ROOTS OF CON- SENSUS: THE POSTWAR GENERATION AND THE NEW PROSPERITY

Chapter 1 THE HERO IN GRAY FLANNEL

The title that writer SLOAN WILSON (1920-   ), a war veteran, former TIME journalist, and public-relations man, chose for his best-selling novel of 1955, The Man in the Gray Flannel Suit, *caught popular attention upon publication and seems in retrospect to represent an era when the typical young American presumably was a faceless, silent business executive intent on success in corporate management. Wilson's central figure actually is intensely human and, characteristic of his generation, only to be understood against the background of his shattering wartime experiences. "Tom Rath," moreover, while cautiously willing to rise on Madison Avenue, to foster his own interests, and to promote progress in his community through a real-estate development, in the end deliberately quit the race for success with the generous assistance of his boss. Wilson's novel occasionally reflects elements of literary protest but it is essentially a story of affirmation not alienation, with a quiet hero and a happy ending rather than an anti-hero succumbing in defeat or despair.*

. . . . The next morning, Tom put on his best suit, a freshly cleaned and pressed gray flannel. On his way to work he stopped in Grand Central Station to buy a clean white handkerchief and to have his shoes shined. During his luncheon hour he set out to visit the United Broadcasting Corporation. As he walked across Rockefeller Plaza, he thought wryly of the days when he and Betsy had assured each other that money didn't matter. They had told each other that when they were married, before the war, and during the war they had repeated it in long letters. "The important thing is to find a kind of work you really like, and something that is useful," Betsy had written him. "The money doesn't matter."

The hell with that, he thought. The real trouble is that up to now we've been kidding ourselves. We might as well admit that what we want is a big house and a new car and trips to Florida in the winter, and plenty of life insurance. When you come right down to it, a man with three children has no damn right to say that money doesn't matter."

There were eighteen elevators in the lobby of the United Broadcasting building. They were all brass colored and looked as though they were made of money. The receptionist in the personnel office was a breathtakingly beautiful girl with money-colored hair—a sort of copper gold. "Yes?" she said.

"I want to apply for a position in the public-relations department."

"If you will sit down in the reception room, I'll arrange an interview for you," she said.

The company had a policy of giving all job applicants an interview. Every year about twenty thousand people, most of them wildly unqualified, applied for jobs there, and it was considered poor public relations to turn them away too abruptly. Beyond the receptionist's desk was a huge waiting room. A rich wine-red carpet was on the floor, and there were dozens of heavy leather armchairs filled with people nervously smoking cigarettes. On the walls were enormous colored photographs of the company's leading radio and television stars. They were all youthful, handsome, and unutterably rich-appearing as they smiled down benignly on the job applicants. Tom picked a chair directly beneath a picture of a big-bosomed blonde. He had to wait only about twenty minutes before the receptionist told him that a Mr. Everett would see him. Mr. Everett's office was a cubicle with walls of opaque glass brick, only about three times as big as a priest's confessional. Everett himself was a man about Tom's age and was also dressed in a gray flannel suit. The uniform of the day, Tom thought. Somebody must have put out an order.

"I understand that you are interested in a position in the public-relations department," Everett said.

"I just want to explore the situation," Tom replied. "I already have a good position with the Schanenhauser Foundation, but I'm considering a change."

It took Everett only about a minute to size Tom up as a "possibility." He gave him a long printed form to fill out and told him he'd hear from the United Broadcasting Corporation in a few days. Tom spent almost an hour filling out all the pages of the form, which, among other things, required a list of the childhood diseases he had had and the names of countries he had visited. When he had finished, he gave it to the girl with the hair of copper gold and rang for one of the golden elevators to take him down. . . .

Walker's outer office was impressive. As soon as Tom saw it, he knew he was being seriously considered for a job, and maybe a pretty good one. Walker had two secretaries, one chosen for looks apparently, and one for utility. A pale-yellow carpet lay on the floor, and there was a yellow leather armchair for callers. Walker himself was closeted in an inner office which was separated from the rest of the room by a partition of opaque glass brick.

The utilitarian secretary told Tom to wait. It was extremely quiet. Neither of the two girls was typing, and although each had two telephones on her desk and an interoffice communication box, there was no ringing or buzzing. Both the secretaries sat reading typewritten sheets in black notebooks. After Tom had waited about half an hour, the pretty secretary, with no audible or visible cue, suddenly looked up brightly and said, "Mr. Walker will see you now. Just open the door and go in."

Tom opened the door and saw a fat, pale man sitting in a high-backed upholstered chair behind a kidney-shaped desk with nothing on it but a blotter and pen. He was in his shirt sleeves, and he weighed about two hundred and fifty pounds. His face was as white as a marshmallow. He didn't stand up when Tom came in, but he smiled. It was a surprisingly warm, spontaneous smile, as though he had unexpectedly recognized an old friend. "Thomas Rath?" he said. "Sit down! Make yourself comfortable! Take off your coat!"

Tom thanked him and, although it wasn't particularly warm, took off his coat. There wasn't anyplace to put it, so, sitting down in the comfortable chair in front of Walker's desk, he laid the coat awkwardly acorss his lap.

"I've read the application forms you filled out, and it seems to me you might be qualified for a new position we may have opening up here," Walker said. "There are just a few questions I want to ask you." He was still smiling. Suddenly he touched a button on the arm of his chair and the back of the chair dropped, allowing him to recline, as though he were in an airplane seat. Tom could see only his face across the top of the desk.

"You will excuse me," Walker said, still smiling. "The doctor says I must get plenty of rest, and this is the way I do it."

Tom couldn't think of anything more appropriate to say than, "It looks comfortable. . . ."

"Why do you want to work for the United Broadcasting Corporation?" Walker asked abruptly.

"It's a good company . . . " Tom began hesitantly, and was suddenly impatient at the need for hypocrisy. The sole reason he wanted to work for United Broadcasting was that he thought he might be able to make a lot of money there fast, but he felt he couldn't say that. It was sometimes considered fashionable for the employees of foundations to say that they were in it for the money, but people were supposed to work at advertising agencies and broadcasting companies for spiritual reasons.

"I believe," Tom said, "that television is developing into the greatest medium for mass education and entertainment. It has always fascinated me, and I would like to work with it. . . ."

"What kind of salary do you have in mind?" Walker asked. Tom hadn't expected the question that soon. Walker was still smiling.

"The salary isn't the primary consideration with me," Tom said, trying desperately to come up with stock answers to stock questions. "I'm mainly interested in finding something useful and worth while to do. I have personal responsibilities, however, and I would hope that something could be worked out to enable me to meet them. . . ."

"Of course," Walker said, beaming more cheerfully than ever. "I understand you applied for a position in the public-relations department. Why did you choose that?"

Because I heard there was an opening, Tom wanted to say, but quickly thought better of it and substituted a halting avowal of life-long interest in public relations. "I think my experience in working with *people* at the Schanenhauser Foundation would be helpful," he concluded lamely.

"I see," Walker said kindly. There was a short silence before he added, "Can you write?"

"I do most of the writing at the Schanenhauser Foundation," Tom said. "The annual report to the trustees is my job, and so are most of the reports on individual projects. I used to be editor of my college paper."

"That sounds fine," Walker said casually. "I have a little favor I want to ask of you. I want you to write me your autobiography."

"What?" Tom asked in astonishment.

"Nothing very long," Walker said. "Just as much as you can manage to type out in an hour. One of my girls will give you a room with a typewriter."

"Is there anything in particular you want me to tell you about?"

"Yourself," Walker said, looking hugely pleased. "Explain yourself to me. Tell me what kind of person you are. Explain why we should hire you."

"I'll try," Tom said weakly.

"You'll have precisely an hour," Walker said. "You see, this is a device I use in employing people—I find it most helpful. For this particular job, I have twenty or thirty applicants. It's hard to tell from a brief interview whom to choose, so I ask them all to write about themselves for an hour. You'd be surprised how revealing the results are. . . ."

He paused, still smiling. Tom said nothing.

"Just a few hints," Walker continued. "Write anything you want, but at the end of your last page, I'd like you to finish this sentence: 'The most significant fact about me is . . . '"

"The most significant fact about me is . . . " Tom repeated idiotically.

"The results, of course, will be entirely confidential." Walker lifted a bulky arm and inspected his wrist watch. "It's now five minutes to twelve," he concluded. "I'll expect your paper on my desk at precisely one o'clock."

Tom stood up, put on his coat, said, "Thank you," and went out of the room. The utilitarian secretary already had a stack of typewriting paper ready for him. She led him to a small room a few doors down the hall in which were a typewriter and a hard office chair. There was a large clock on the wall. The room had no windows. Across the ceiling was a glaring fluorescent light which made the bare white plaster walls look yellow. The secretary walked out without a word, shutting the door silently behind her.

Tom sat down in the chair, which had been designed for a stenographer and was far too small for him. Son of a bitch, he thought—I guess the laws about cruel and unusual punishment don't apply to personnel men. He tried to think of something to write, but all he could remember was Betsy and the drab little house and the need to buy a new washing machine, and the time he had thrown a vase that cost forty dollars against the wall. "The most significant fact about me is that I once threw a vase costing forty dollars against a wall." That would be as sensible as anything else he could think of, but he doubted whether it would get him the job. He thought of Janey saying, "It isn't *fair!*" and the worn linoleum on the kitchen floor. "The most significant fact about me is . . . " It was a stupid sentence to ask a man to finish.

I have children, he thought—that's probably the most significant fact about me, the only one that will have much importance for long. Anything about a man can be summed up in numbers. Thomas R. Rath, thirty-three years old, making seven thousand dollars a year, owner of a 1939 Ford, a six-room house, and ten thousand dollars' worth of G. I. Life Insurance which, in case of his death, would pay his widow about forty dollars a month. Six feet one and a half inches tall; weight, 198 pounds. He served four and a half years in the Army, most of it in Europe and the rest in the South Pacific.

Another statistical fact came to him then, a fact which he knew would be ridiculously melodramatic to put into an application for a job at United Broadcasting Corporation, or to think about at all. He hadn't thought about this for a long while. It wasn't a thing he had deliberately tried to forget—he simply hadn't thought about it for quite a few years. It was the unreal-sounding, probably irrelevant, but quite accurate fact that he had killed seventeen men.

It had been during the war, of course. He had been a paratrooper. Lots of other people had killed more men than he had. Lots of bomber crews and artillerymen had, but, of course, they never really knew it. Lots of infantrymen and lots of paratroopers had, and most of them knew it. Plenty of men had been dropped behind the enemy lines, as Tom had been on five different occasions, and they had had to do some of their killing silently, with blackjacks and knives. They had known what they were doing, and most of them were healthy enough not to be morbid about it, and not to be proud of it, and not to be ashamed of it. Such things were merely part of the war, the war before the Korean one. It was no longer fashionable to talk about the war, and certainly it had never been fashionable to talk about the number of men one had killed. Tom couldn't forget the number, "seventeen," but it didn't seem real any more; it was just a small, isolated statistic that nobody wanted. His mind went blank. Suddenly the word "Maria" flashed into it.

"The most significant fact about me is that . . ."

Nonsense, he thought, and brought himself back to the present with a jerk. Only masochists can get along without editing their own memories. Maria was a girl he had known in Italy during the war, a long time ago, and he never thought about her any more, just as he never thought about the seventeen men he had killed. It wasn't always easy to forget, but it was certainly necessary to try.

"The most significant fact about me is that for four and a half years my profession was jumping out of airplanes with a gun, and now I want to go into public relations."

That probably wouldn't get him the job, Tom thought. "The most significant fact about me is that I detest the United Broadcasting Corporation, with all its soap operas, commercials, and yammering studio audiences, and the only reason I'm willing to spend my life in such a ridiculous enterprise is that I want to buy a more expensive house and a better brand of gin."

That certainly wouldn't get him the job.

"The most significant fact about me is that I've become a cheap cynic."

That would not be apt to get him the job.

"The most significant fact about me is that as a young man in college, I played the mandolin incessantly. I, champion mandolin player, am applying to you for a position in the public-relations department!"

That would not be likely to get him far. Impatiently he sat down at the typewriter and glanced at his wrist watch. It was a big loud-ticking wrist watch with a black face, luminous figures, and a red sweep hand that rapidly ticked off the seconds. He had bought it years ago at an Army post exchange and had worn it all through the war. The watch was the closest thing to a good-luck charm he had ever had, although he never thought of it as such. Now it was more reassuring to look at than the big impersonal clock on the wall, though both said it was almost twelve-thirty. So far he had written nothing. What the hell, he thought. I was a damn fool to think I wanted to work here anyway. Then he thought of Betsy asking, as she would be sure to, "Did you get the job? How did it go?" And he decided to try.

"Anybody's life can be summed up in a paragraph," he wrote. "I was born on November 20, 1920, in my grandmother's house in South Bay, Connecticut. I was graduated from Covington Academy in 1937, and from Harvard College in 1941. I spent four and a half years in the Army, reaching the rank of captain. Since 1946, I have been employed as an assistant to the director of the Schanenhauser Foundation. I live in Westport, Connecticut, with my wife and three children. From the point of view of the United Broadcasting Corporation, the most significant fact about me is that I am applying for a position in its public-relations department, and after an initial period of learning, I probably would do a good job. I will be glad to answer any questions which seem relevant, but after considerable thought, I have decided that I do not wish to attempt an autobiography as part of an application for a job."

He typed this paragraph neatly in the precise center of a clean piece of paper, added his name and address, and carried it into Walker's office. It was only quarter to one, and Walker was obviously surprised to see him. "You've still got fifteen minutes!" he said.

"I've written all I think is necessary," Tom replied, and handed him the almost empty page.

Walker read it slowly, his big pale face expressionless. When he had finished it, he dropped it into a drawer. "We'll let you know our decision in a week or so," he said. . . .

On the evening of October 8, Tom and Betsy Rath went to the Town Hall in South Bay to attend the public hearing on the proposed new school. The town hall was stuffy, and the people filing in from the commuting trains looked bored. The chair on which Tom sat was hard, and he was tired. He squirmed restlessly. Why is it that important public issues always have to be decided in places like this? he thought. Somehow the hard chairs, the smoky room, and the rumpled coats of the weary commuters didn't seem to be the right props for stirring decisions about anything. "How long do you think this meeting will take?" he asked Betsy.

At five minutes after eight, Bernstein, who had been appointed moderator, walked out on a raised platform at the front of the hall. He foresaw an evening of bitter argument, and his stomach was already beginning to ache. Sitting behind a wooden table, he picked up a gavel and tapped it lightly. Gradually the big auditorium quieted down. "Good evening," Bernstein said. "We have gathered here for a hearing on an eight-hundred-thousand-dollar bond issue which has been proposed for a new elementary school, and which we will vote on a week from today. The call for this meeting has been duly published in the newspaper, and I hereby make a motion that we dispense with reading it."

"Motion seconded," someone from the audience called.

"All in favor say 'Aye,' " Bernstein said.

"Aye!" the audience thundered.

"Nay?" Bernstein asked.

"No!" a lone, derisive voice called, and the audience laughed.

"The Ayes have it," Bernstein said, and thought, They seem good humored, but a crowd's laughter can be a symptom of tension. He cleared his throat and said, "To begin the proceedings, Dr. Clyde Eustace, Superintendent of Schools, will tell why he believes a new elementary school is necessary."

Eustace, who had been sitting in the front row, climbed to the platform. He was a large man, but his voice was surprisingly soft. "Ladies and gentlemen, it's very simple," he said. "Although the present elementary school building is badly overcrowded, the welfare of our children is only one question to be discussed tonight. Another basic issue is whether this town should be allowed to grow any more. If you build houses you have to build schools. The main thing I want to point out is that if you decide to vote *no* on this school, you are voting against any further development of this community, and . . . "

A tall, gray-haired man in the front row stood up. "I'm willing to fight it out on those grounds," he said.

Bernstein banged his gavel. "Dr. Eustace has the floor!" he said sharply.

Betsy glanced at Tom. "Who's that?" she asked.

"Parkington's his name," Tom replied. "He was an old friend of Grandmother's—they used to feud all the time."

"Eustace doesn't have to say any more," Parkington persisted. "He's named the basic issue."

"Dr. Eustace will have the floor until I as moderator recognize someone else, and I have not yet recognized you, Mr. Parkington," Bernstein said firmly, and banged his gavel again. "Dr. Eustace, please continue."

Parkington sat down. Eustace went on to give many facts and figures about the need for a new school. He talked too long, and the tone of his voice became monotonous. As soon as he was through, Parkington stood up again.

"All right, Mr. Parkington, you may have the floor now," Bernstein said.

"Let's just go back to what Dr. Eustace said a few moments ago," Parkington began in a deep voice. "If you vote *no* on this school, you vote against further development of this community—and, if I may so so, against further deterioration. What I'm trying to tell everyone here tonight is that's exactly what you should do."

"That's bad for our housing project," Tom whispered to Betsy. "Parkington's nuts, but he's pretty powerful around here."

"This has always been a good town, a beautiful town," Parkington continued passionately. "I was born and brought up here. I've never been able to understand why people move here because they like the place and then start to change it. This new school will send taxes up. That will drive the owners of big estates out. If the big estates are broken up, housing projects will come in. Housing projects bring more children than they do money. The average small house owner pays the town only about a third of what it costs to educate his children. Who's going to make up the difference?"

There was a rising murmur from the audience, and several people tried to speak at once. Bernstein slammed the table with his gavel. "Mr. Parkington still has the floor," he said. "Do you wish to continue, Mr. Parkington?"

"Yes," said Parkington. "I just want to point out that if this school is built, it won't be six month before another one is needed. I've heard a rumor that the old Rath estate is going to be made into a housing development. I'd like to come right out and ask Mr. Rath about that now. I know he's here tonight, because I saw him come in. He's sitting right there in one of the back rows. How about it, Tom? Aren't you just waiting for this school to go through, so you can get permission from the Zoning Board to cut up your land?"*

"Mr. Rath, would you care to comment?" Bernstein asked. His stomach was hurting quite badly now.

Slowly Tom stood up. There was a rustling sound throughout the auditorium as people twisted in their seats to see him. He glanced at Betsy and saw she looked nervous. Mechanically he smiled at her. The hall seemed astonishingly quiet, and all faces were turned toward him. His mouth felt dry. "I didn't come prepared to give a talk . . . " he began lamely.

Somewhere in the crowd there was a snicker, which quickly grew into laughter. Bernstein tapped his gavel. "Mr. Rath, please step to the front of the hall," he said.

Awkwardly Tom edged his way to the aisle. The walk to the front of the auditorium seemed endless. Then he was on the platform facing the crowd, and the laughter subsided. The upturned faces blurred. It doesn't really matter, he thought. Here goes nothing. It will be interesting to see what happens. "All right," he said suddenly in a firm voice, "the rumor is true. I plan to ask the Zoning Board for permission to start a housing project."

He paused, and the hall was utterly silent. He couldn't find Betsy's face in the crowd. He took a deep breath. "I don't want my plans for a housing project to hurt the chances for this new school," he said. "They ought to be decided as separate issues. A new school is needed right now. I've got two children in the old one, and I've seen it—it's terrible. Let's get the new school first and fight the battle of my housing project later."

"But the school is an opening wedge!" Parkington interrupted. Bernstein banged his gavel.

"Mr. Parkington," Tom continued, "I think I see your point of view. I was born in South Bay too, and I like the town the way it is. As a matter of fact, I liked it even better the way it used to be, didn't you? It was prettier before the houses went up on the golf course. What I'm trying to say is, the town *is* changing, and we can't take a vote to stop change. If the Zoning Board lets me start a housing project, I'll do everything possible to keep it from being unsightly, or a financial drain on the town, but I don't promise to keep my grandmother's house and land unchanged. That's impossible. And I hope you won't leave the school we have today unchanged. As it stands today, it's a disgrace to all of us."

There was mild applause as Tom stepped down from the platform. Almost immediately Parkington was on his feet. "I just want to warn everybody here that breaking up the Rath estate is just the beginning," he said. "If we don't hold taxes down, other big estates will go. I've just heard that the big place the president of a broadcasting company built down by the water has been placed on the market."

"I know a little about that, and it doesn't have anything to do with schools or taxes," Tom said quickly.

"Maybe," Parkington replied, "but if the big estates go, and we keep on building schools, our taxes will be doubled!"

"I don't think the big estates will go just because we build a new school, and even if they do, I don't think we're so poor and so helpless we can't educate our children," Tom said.

"That sounds fine," Parkington retorted heatedly, "but I'm telling you here and now that if we replace the big estates with housing projects, South Bay will become slum within ten years—a slum, I tell you, a slum!"

He paused, and the silence was impressive.

"I don't agree with you," Tom said quietly. "We won't let the town become a slum." He started walking toward the back of the hall to rejoin Betsy. Immediately a dozen people were on their feet asking Bernstein for permission to be heard. Antonio Bugala, the contractor, began an impassioned plea for increased business opportunities. For more than an hour the argument raged back and forth, the voices becoming louder and more strident. Tom glanced at Betsy. She looked scared. How curious, he thought, that we should be so dependent—that so much of our future should depend on what all these shouting people decide. His head started to ache, and he longed for the cool air outside.

Finally there was a pause. "Does anyone have anything more to add about the construction of a new school?" Bernstein asked wearily.

Parkington jumped to his feet again immediately. "To sum it all up, a vote for a school is a vote for a housing project Tom Rath admits he's planning," he said. "That's a vote to make this town a slum!"

Bernstein raised his gavel. "If there are no more opinions to be heard . . . " he said.

"A slum!" Parkington repeated portentously.

"Wait a minute!" Betsy called impetuously, and suddenly found herself on her feet. Tom looked at her in astonishment and saw that her face was flushed.

"Mrs. Rath has the floor," Bernstein said.

For an instant Betsy hesitated. "I'm sorry," she said. "I just didn't want this meeting to end with the word *slum*."

The audience was attentive.

"The children need a new school," Betsy continued. "Don't let our housing project be used as a weapon against . . . "

"This will be only the beginning . . . " Parkington interrupted.

"Mr. Parkington!" Betsy cut in with remarkable self-possession. "I don't think that growth will necessarily hurt the town. And although I may be taking advantage of being a woman, I refuse to let you have the last word!"

The audience laughed, and although Parkington said something no one could hear him. Bernstein banged his gavel. Gradually the hall quieted. "I think we've heard the full expression of all relevant opinions," Bernstein said. "I remind you that a week from today we vote on this issue. This meeting stands adjourned." . . .

Chapter 2 THE DISCOVERY OF A CHANGED AMERICA

FREDERICK LEWIS ALLEN *(1890-1954) was for many years the editor of the* Century *and* Harper's, *but best known to several generations of college students for his immensely readable and perceptive social histories, notably* Only Yesterday, *an astute survey of the 1920's. In 1952 Allen published* The Big Change: America Transforms Itself, 1900-1950, *in which he pointed out to his readers that the United States had not sunk back into economic depression after the war as so many had anticipated, but that there were clear signs of increasing prosperity, that important and gratifying social progress was occurring, and that the nation was "not evolving toward* socialism, *but* past socialism." *There is revealed in Allen's book not only his usual humor but an air of discovery, his feeling of pleasure over the turn of events, and his shrewd sense of significant social changes. The book also contributed to a widespread reconsideration in the 1950's of the character of American corporate enterprise and of the entire American experience, and thus Allen helped to give rise to the new intellectual school of "consensus" that played down conflict and crisis in the nation's history.*

. . . . But there was no postwar depression. And all this time the uneasy American conscience was steadily at work. The result was that the postwar years saw a change that would have seemed unbelievable only a decade earlier.

A series of Supreme Court decisions set aside many of the laws and practices which had kept Negroes from the polls and from educational opportunity. One decision weakened the force of racially restrictive real-estate covenants. A number of Southern states repealed the poll-tax laws which had prevented great numbers of poor people, white and black, from voting; in the election of 1948 over a million Southern Negroes went to the polls. The Air Force and Navy officially ended segregation and the Army modified its former segregation practices. The pressure of

Frederick Lewis Allen, *The Big Change: America Transforms Itself, 1900-1950* (New York: Harper & Brothers 1952), pp. 181-183, 199-201, 209, 211-213, 225, 252, 290-293. Copyright 1952 by Frederick Lewis Allen. Reprinted by permission. Footnotes omitted.

"fair employment" laws in several Northern states, combined with the eagerness of many employers to set an example of enlightened employment policy, brought about the entry of colored workers in many fields of employment new to them. In New York, for example, anybody returning to the city after a long absence would have been struck by the large numbers of colored men and women in the midtown busses and on the midtown streets, traveling to jobs that had previously been for whites only, or to shop in stores where colored customers had previously been few and far between. In Northern and Western cities generally there was a noticeable breakdown of Jim Crow restrictions in hotels, restaurants, and theaters.

Ever since the nineteen-twenties there had been a rising appreciation, among intellectuals, of the Negro contributions to the arts, and especially to jazz music; and as time went on there developed among the more ardent students of jazz such a reverence for the pioneering contributions of the original jazz musicians of New Orleans and Memphis, and for the inheritors of the traditions of Basin Street and Beale Street, that men like Duke Ellington and Louis Armstrong found themselves the objects of a deep and deferential respect among thousand of music lovers. Meanwhile, in quite another area, the statesmanship and dignity of Ralph Bunche, as mediator in the Near East, was winning for him the admiration of innumerable whites. But still more important for Negro prestige, because it involved such an enormous public, was the prowess of Joe Louis, the great heavy-weight champion, of whom Jimmy Cannon said that he was a credit to his race—the human race; and also the performance of a number of colored baseball players after the Jim Crow restrictions in professional baseball were broken down in the late nineteen-forties. Not only did the remarkable playing and exemplary behavior of men like Jackie Robinson make the earlier color line in baseball seem preposterous to the fans, but by 1950 most of the enthusiasts for baseball seemed to choose their favorite players with almost no regard for the color line; and so carefully did radio reporters of baseball games refrain from mentioning the color of the players that there were actually stay-at-home fans who could tell you Roy Campanella's approximate batting average but were not aware that he was a Negro.

"Probably the most important thing that has happened in the United States in the field of race relations," wrote Mrs. Eleanor Roosevelt, "is that so many things are now taken for granted where the integration of the two races is concerned. This was brought home to me at the Inauguration of 1945 in the White House when a group of newspaper women who had been watching the receiving line came to me at the end of the day and said: 'Do you realize what twelve years have done? If at the 1933 reception a number of colored people had gone down the line and mixed with everyone else in the way they did today, every paper in the country would have reported it. We do not even think it is news and none of us will mention it."

No longer did magazines, newspapers, and moving pictures show Negroes almost exclusively as comic or menial characters. Those ancient stereotypes had been largely eliminated.

Most striking of all the changes, perhaps, was a new attitude on the part of younger white Americans, both North and South—a very widespread resolve to accept Negroes as people without regard to their color. This attitude was manifest when, following Supreme Court decisions, a number of universities in the southern and border states admitted Negroes to unsegregated standing. University administrators were uneasy: would some hothead whites among the students raise a ruckus? Up to the end of 1951 there had been no ruckus anywhere. Uniformly, the students took the innovation in their stride. . . .

During the year 1932 a huddle of social scientists put the finishing touches on a massive study of American life which they called *Recent Social Changes*, and in this book some of them made cautious estimates of the probable increase in the future population of the country. Noting that the rate of growth appeared to be slowing down, they figured that a "continuation of present trends" would produce a 1940 population of 132 or 133 millions. In the event they were not far wrong; when the year 1940 rolled round, the actual figure proved to be a trifle smaller—presumably because of the discouragements of the Great Depression—yet only a trifle: it was 131,669,275. But on the same tentative basis the social scientists made a prediction for 1950, and on this one they were spectacularly wrong. Their prediction: between 140½ and 145 millions (which, you will agree, allowed considerable leeway for error). The actual 1950 figures: 150,697,361 people—more than five millions more than their outside estimate! There had been a huge, unexpected, and altogether astonishing increase.

The chief reason for the increase was a big jump in the birth rate during the nineteen-forties. To ascribe this flatly to "war and prosperity," as some people have done, seems a little oversimple; for World War I had brought no such big bulge, and during the reasonably prosperous nineteen-twenties the birthrate had not risen but had declined a little. Yet undeniably the draft regulations, deferring husbands with children, were a factor. Another was the natural tendency of young people facing the prospect of being separated for months or years—or perhaps forever—to plunge into marriage in a hurry. Still another was the eagerness of young men returning from the notably undomestic life of the armed services, and of girls who had been waiting for them, to want to begin to enjoy domesticity just as soon as possible, with terminal pay and in many cases the G. I. Bill of Rights to help finance the venture. And at a time when wars and rumors of wars seemed to jeopardize one's career and threaten one's very life, there was not only a human need for seizing whatever satisfactions were within reach but also, perhaps, a desire to make some sort of contribution to the future, to perpetuate one's blood—or if not an outright desire (since most births are in some degree accidental) at least a slackening of the resolution not to perpetuate it for the time being.

In any case the birth rate, which—after a long decline—in the nineteen-thirties had hovered in the neighborhood of 17 or 18 per thousand of population, went to

20.9 in 1942 and 21.5 in 1943: declined a trifle to 20.2 in 1944 and 19.6 in 1945 (when a good many million potential fathers were in Europe or on Pacific islands or at sea); and then rose abruptly to 23.3 in 1946 and 25.8 in 1947—after which it declined, but only very slightly, to 24.2 in 1948, 24.1 in 1949, and 23.5 in 1950.

Surely here was a very interesting reaction to the dislocations and carnage of war. It came at a time when many of the more articulate intellectuals appeared to have reached the conclusion that the hazardousness of life, the helplessness of the individual in the grip of blind destiny, and the general decline of firm convictions as to the value of human effort, were reducing mankind to despair. What happened to the birth rate would seem to give grounds for wondering whether the population in general was not taking a cheerier view of the future. Even among American college graduates as a group (who for a long time had been reproved for not reproducing themselves) the trend in the birth rate was upward; records of the alumni and alumnae of 167 colleges showed that the class of '41 had produced, by 1951, more children per graduate than the class of '36 had done when ten years out.

Was the institution of the family taking on a new lease of life in America? This notion may seem odd to one who notes that while the marriage rate, which had lagged during the Great Depression, rose during and after the war to a lofty peak in 1946, so did the divorce rate. But the large number of divorces at that time was surely due in part to repentance at leisure from hasty wartime alliances. For if it is true, as a cynic has said, that proximity and opportunity are responsible for most marriages, so a lack of proximity and a variety of opportunity will break up many marriages. And even though during the rest of the nineteen-forties the divorce rate remained higher than in prewar years—2.6 per thousand population in 1949, for example, as against the high figure of 4.3 in 1946 and a mere 2 in 1940, 1.6 in 1930, 1.6 in 1920, 0.9 in 1910, and 0.7 in 1900—this gave evidence, perhaps, of a declining conviction that marriages should be durable, but not of any doubt that they were desirable.

The figures seem to bear out one's impression that most American young people of the nineteen-forties had no such cynical or disillusioned reservations about marrying and bringing up a family as had possessed many of the bright young people of earlier decades. They did not want to prolong indefinitely the delights of single adventure. They did not regard marriage as a bourgeois expedient for enforcing a conventional monogamy upon free spirits. Nor did they, despite many warnings of the forthcoming collapse of civilization, regard with undue dismay adding to the number of human creatures who must allegedly confront that collapse. No, they wanted to marry and have babies, preferably in a ranch-type house with a dishwashing machine for the joint use of husband and wife, and with a TV set which would entertain them right beside the conjugal hearth. They had been around a lot and had decided that east, west, home was best. . . .

As we enter upon the second half of the twentieth century and pause to take stock of our situation, let us look to see, first, what has happened to the gap that once yawned so widely between rich and poor.

In money terms—income terms—the change has not been overwhelming. There are still islands of deep poverty in the United States, and there are families and individuals by the millions who through illness, age, adversity, or marginal ability, live on the ragged edge of want. And the average represents nothing like affluence. Yet even so, what has happened over half a century, but most impressively since 1940, has been striking enough to be described by the definitely unhysterical director of research of the National Bureau of Economic Research as "one of the great social revolutions of history.". . .

. . . . Now let us look for a moment at the lowest of these groups: the 10.6 per cent of the families (or thereabouts), and also the individuals, who are living on annual incomes of less than $1,000. Who are they?

They include, to begin with, some farmers and private businessmen who have simply had a bad year—have had to sell crops or goods at a loss, let us say. But some or most of these have savings enough to tide them along. (No grinding poverty there, in most cases.) They include a great number of rural poor: people working poor and worn-out land, tenants, sharecroppers. (A good many of these—we don't know how many—may be able to raise enough food for their own use so as to manage somehow on even a grimly small money income.) Another group, not quite so large, consists of old people, who in some cases have families depending on their meager savings or earnings, and in other cases are fending for themselves alone, with or without old-age relief. (One out of every four families dependent on elderly people and two out of three single elderly men and women had to get along in 1948 on less than $20 a week, said Robert L. Heilbroner in a study of American poverty in *Harper's Magazine* for June, 1950.) Others of the lowest group are victims of broken families—women, for example, who have been divorced or deserted and are unable to support themselves properly. Some are disabled people—the crippled, the mentally ill. (Many of these, to quote Mr. Heilbroner, "will be wards of the community as long as they live.") Some, probably, are chronic ne'er-do-wells, useless derelicts of society, seldom hired and then not for long. One should add that among the rural poor and the stranded old people and such-like a disproportionate number are Negroes.

Step up into the next lowest rank of poverty, the group with family or individual incomes of between $1,000 and $2,000 a year, and we find more businessmen who have been encountering tough sledding, more marginal farmers, more old people, more divorced or deserted wives, more disabled people, more marginal laborers who have been laid off again and again, and also some members of another group: those whose wages, even in this time of plenty, have been so low as to keep them in a constant struggle with poverty. Again, among most of these groups there is an unduly large representation of Negroes.

Perhaps the most striking thing about the make-up of these two groups, comprising the lowest third of the nation, income-wise, is that—with the partial exception of the Negroes whose special situation I have discussed in Chapter 12—these are not "the masses." They are not a proletariat. They are a great number of people, very widely scattered, who are in very different sorts of trouble, economic and otherwise.

They may range all the way from the elderly man who lives so neatly and proudly that you would never guess, to see him, that he sometimes goes hungry, and the upstanding farmer whose crops for this year have been ruined by storm, to the bum who panhandles to buy himself another drink, and the moron who hasn't the wit to hold a job. Our facilities for helping these misfits and victims of adversity are far from ideal, heaven knows, but they are far more adequate than they were at the beginning of the century. And there are no such huge pools of mass misery as existed then.

During the Depression Stuart Chase once wrote something to the effect that in a fluid society there would always be people climbing up the economic staircase and others tumbling down it, but that if it was a decent society there should be some way of preventing the latter from falling all the way to the cellar. What with the helpfulness of relatives and neighbors, and the efforts of private charitable organizations, and our city and county relief organizations, we succeed nowadays in catching most of them at the ground floor.

It is when we examine the next two or three brackets—those representing incomes of $2,000 to $10,000—that we encounter the central fact of our present prosperity. This is that millions upon millions of families have risen out of the under-$2,000 class and the $2,000-$3,000 class and have climbed a bracket or two. These fortunate families have been getting their money from a wide variety of occupations; among them have been farmers, office workers, professional people, semiskilled and skilled industrial workers; but it is the industrial workers who as a group have done best—people such as a steelworker's family who used to live on $2,500 and now are getting $4,500, or the highly skilled machine-tool operator's family who used to have $3,000 and now can spend an annual $5,500 or more. Consider a single salient statistic: that the *average* earnings of workers in all manufacturing industries in America in 1950 were $59.33 a week. During the past decade these earnings, as they climbed, have been pursued by rising prices, but on the average they have kept well ahead.

What do these figures mean in human terms? That millions of families in our industrial cities and towns, and on the farms, have been lifted from poverty or near-poverty to a status where they can enjoy what has been traditionally considered a middle-class way of life: decent clothes for all, an opportunity to buy a better automobile, install an electric refrigerator, provide the housewife with a decently attractive kitchen, go to the dentist, pay insurance premiums, and so on indefinitely.

Whether these industrial workers, farmers, and other assorted people have been the ones most deserving of such a lift in fortune is uncertain. One might have wished that intellectual workers—teachers for example—had been among the principal beneficiaries of the new order. (They certainly have not.) Nevertheless the effect upon the rest of us of the dwindling away of what used to be the lower class has been impressive. For as the families which have moved up a bracket or two have been able to buy more goods, their expanded purchasing power has given an immense lift to business in general. America has become more prosperous by making the poor less poor. . . .

And what is the result? Both the rich man's fourteen-year-old son, who dismays his conservative parents by trying to talk like Humphrey Bogart, and the truck driver's son, who cherishes the same hope, will grow up to be more like their idols—and thus, more like one another—than they would have otherwise. And something else happens. Half a century ago a coal miner who found himself at a fashionable restaurant would not have had the faintest notion of how to behave; nowadays he has only to ask himself, "How would Gregory Peck do it?" In short, the social distance between the extremes of American society is shrinking.

Whenever I think of this change, I think of something I saw not long ago in New York City. A street was being torn up for repairs, and while the workmen were standing waiting for the arrival of new equipment, one of them, who had in his hands an iron rod presumably used for prying off manhole covers, was enjoying a little relaxation. I looked twice to see what he was doing with that rod. He was practicing a graceful golf stroke. . . .

The Great Depression had much to do with it. The top men of America's big corporations remember the doghouse which they inhabited in those days; and though some of the elder ones are still unreconstructed Washington-haters, and there is hardly a man in authority today who does not on occasion splutter at some of the restrictions—and monumental paper work—imposed upon him by the government, a great many of the younger and more nimble-minded of them have acquired a genuine distaste for the shenanigans of the nineteen-twenties, a firm intention not to butt their heads against the political and social facts of life as their predecessors did, and a hard-learned but unfeigned awareness of the principle that, in the long run, as Peter F. Drucker has put it, "No policy is likely to benefit the business itself unless it also benefits the society." The war had something to do with the change, too, bringing together as it did businessmen, government men, labor leaders, physical scientists, social scientists, and assorted professional men in government undertakings in which they learned to appreciate one another's competence and point of view. I do not mean that our business executives have put on haloes; I prefer the way in which the attitude of these men was described by Ralph Coghlan of the St. Louis *Post Dispatch* at the Corning conference of 1951—a conference, by the way, which dealt with "Living in Industrial Civilization," and brought together in a two-day powwow businessmen, sociologists and other scholars, journalists, and government officials, and was staged by a business concern, the Corning Glass Company. Said Mr. Coghlan:

"When I was growing up, the word 'soulless' corporation was a very common term. . . . Well, in my lifetime I have seen a remarkable change in this. I don't know whether it could be said that corporations have obtained souls, but at least they have obtained intelligence." . . .

But the fury of our political campaigns, and the angry disputes over this or that congressional bill, detract our attention from a remarkable fact: that despite the purple language which is tossed about, very few Americans seriously propose any *really wholesale* change in our evolving American system. (And at that, our stormiest debates in recent years have not been over domestic policy but over foreign policy, or over the supposed influence of American Communists and their friends and alleged friends over foreign policy.) There is a large amount of antipathy to the administration in power in Washington. There are numerous people who would like to curb federal power, repeal various laws now on the books, pare down the bureaucracy, minimize relief. There are others who want the government to take on new labors and new powers, like that of running a great medical insurance program. Yet the vast majority of Americans agree that the government should continue to accept an overall responsibility for the satisfactory operation of the national economy; that it should continue to accept responsibility for relief when necessary; that it should supervise and regulate business to *some* extent; that it should subsidize and guarantee various groups to *some* extent—but that it should keep its intervention limited, and should let the great bulk of business remain under private management. The seething debate is over how much of this and how much of that we need, but the area of virtual agreement is very wide; and this includes letting private business remain in private hands.

For we believe we have demonstrated that business can be far more resourcefully and ingeniously run by private managers; and furthermore that these private managers can run most if not all of it with such consideration for the general public welfare that they can achieve for us all that government ownership would bring, plus the efficiency, flexibility, and adventurousness which government ownership would jeopardize—and without the danger of tyranny that government ownership might invite.

In short, there is subconscious agreement among the vast majority of Americans that the United States is not evolving *toward* socialism, but *past* socialism.

I say subconscious agreement because in our conscious thought most of us still seem to be the victims of an old idea that has become a delusion. This is the idea that there is in the world a sort of inevitable trend of progress toward socialism; that people who want the government to do more than it is doing are therefore liberal (if they are polite about it) or radical (if they are aggressive about it); and that people who want the management of business to remain in private hands are therefore conservative (if polite) or reactionary (if aggressive).

Historically there has been ample warrant for this picture of the political spectrum. During the past century or so the principal political changes have been in the direction of getting the government to do more and more for what was thought to be the common weal; and the people who didn't want the government to act, who wanted to dig their heels in and stop it from acting, were rightly known as conservatives. By contrast the people who went whole hog for government intervention, to the point of wanting the government to take over the ownership and operation of the principal private industries, in short the Socialists, were rightly known as radicals; and those who wanted it to take over virtually everything, by violent revolution if necessary, in short the Communists, were rightly known as extreme radicals. But now the United States has been demonstrating pretty convincingly that the system that works best of all, combining most of the genuine advantages of governmental responsibility and of private initiative, and avoiding the disadvantages of each, is one in which governmental intervention is limited and private industry and private associations have a great degree of freedom; and also that one of the mightiest advantages of this system is the way in which it diffuses very widely the decision-making power and the opportunities that go with it. In short, that the direction of progress is now different from that people had supposed it was.

Yet the delusion persists that the trend of the times is toward socialism—and perhaps even toward communism. Though our production, our wealth, our standard of living are the wonder of the world; though Britain under Socialist leadership had to come to us for financial aid; though, as Isabel Lundberg wrote in 1947, we are in a position to offer tangible goods and expert technological services to nations to whom the Russians, for all their loud talk of material benefits, could not offer so much as a shoelace; though our evolved system is potentially the most revolutionary force on earth, nevertheless so fixed in our minds is this delusion that when we face foreign problems we instinctively consider ourselves the natural allies of conservatism, and we tend to behave as if we wanted to stifle the natural hopes of mankind for a decenter way of life. Instinctively we set our faces against change. And preposterously we think of Soviet Russia—which has submerged the historic Communist aim of a better life for the masses of people in an aim of national aggrandizement through barbaric means—as if it and its allied zealots and dupes represented radicalism, represented a disposition of things toward which we ourselves might drift if we did not hold fast against change; as if Soviet Russia were something other than a despotic medievalism which was developed out of a revolutionary attempt to meet the problems of the nineteenth century—problems which we ourselves have long since surmounted.

It is time we rid ourselves of this notion about Russia. It is time we realize that when we battle against communism, we are battling against the past, not against the future. It is time, too, we rid ourselves of the notion that the direction of change at home is toward socialism or communism, and that therefore loyal Americans must stand pat. This notion is a stultifying force in our life. It causes well-meaning people to imagine that anyone with unorthodox ideas must be suspect of subversive intent.

It tends to cramp men's imaginations into a timid conformity. It tends to cramp men's imaginations into a timid conformity. It tends to constrict our generous impulses as people. Combined with the fear of large-scale war, and especially of atomic war, it eats away at our bold confidence in ourselves and our destiny.

We would do better to put it out of our minds, and to realize that our sobering position of leadership in the world is founded upon the fact that we have not stood still. The story of the changes in the contours of American life that we have hammered out in the first half of this twentieth century, is a triumphant story, however harsh may have been some of the experiences in the interim and however obscure may be the shape of the future. We would do well to think of our accomplishment thus far as but the preface to what we may accomplish in the second half of the century if we can continue to invent, improve, and change—and can keep a good heart. The courageous nation, like the courageous man, is not unhappy at the thought of dangers beside the road ahead, but welcomes them as challenges to be faced and overwhelmed along an adventurous course.

Chapter 3 THE MEANING OF ABUNDANCE

DAVID M. POTTER *(1910-1971) was at the time of his premature death one of the most respected of American historians. Then Coe Professor at Stanford University and president of both the American Historical Association and the Organization of American Historians, Potter had established his reputation as a student of the Civil War and of Southern history. In 1954 he published* People of Plenty, *which impressed fellow scholars with its bold use of social-science literature in historical analysis but is perhaps more significant today for the topic pursued in the subtitle:* Economic Abundance and the American Character. *A volume that is strikingly characteristic of the 1950's, when it was widely quoted in scholarly studies of the consensus school and even in business advertising,* People of Plenty *assumes America's bounty, contrasts it to the condition of less-favored lands, argues that the nation had truly been a country with social mobility, and asserts that economic plenty helped shape the national character. Potter concludes his provocative analysis with a suggestive essay on the meaning of abundance for child-rearing in the postwar era.*

. . . . Throughout our national experience, the most varied types of observers have agreed in emphasizing America's bounty. Explorers have marveled at wealth previously undiscovered; travelers have contrasted the riches of America with the scarcity of the lands from which they came; millions of inhabitants of the Old World have responded as immigrants to the lure of the land of plenty, the land of promise, where they could "dwell like kings in fairyland, lords of the soil"; politicians have urged the voter to vote himself a farm or a check for thirty dollars every Thursday or an old age pension or a war bonus, in the confident assurance that the country can meet the draft; exploiters have parried demands for conservation by contending that the sources of our wealth are unlimited; a whole battalion

David M. Potter, *People of Plenty: Economic Abundance and the American Character* (Chicago: The University of Chicago Press, 1954), pp. 80, 91, 93-94, 95-97, 204-208. Copyright 1954 by The University of Chicago. Reprinted by permission. Footnotes omitted.

of statisticians has been deployed on the task of measuring the abundance of natural resources—our cultivable soil, our hydroelectric potential, our timber, our coal, our iron, our copper, our petroleum, our natural gas, and so on; while another battalion has concentrated upon showing how the potential wealth of natural resources has been translated into an unexampled standard of living. . . .

Abundance has influenced American life in many ways, but there is perhaps no respect in which this influence has been more profound than in the forming and strengthening of the American ideal and practice of equality, with all that the ideal has implied for the individual in the way of opportunity to make his own place in society and of emancipation from a system of status. . . .

Today our somewhat disillusioned intellectuals tend to emphasize the fact that the American dream of absolute equality and of universal opportunity was never fulfilled in the literal sense, and they often play up the discrepancy between the realities of American life and the beliefs of the American creed. Discrepancy there is, was, and perhaps ever shall be, and it must be confronted in any analysis; but the recognition of it should not obscure another primary fact, namely, that American conditions, in addition to encouraging a belief in mobility, actually brought about a condition of mobility far more widespread and pervasive than any previous society or previous era of history had ever witnessed. . . .

There is a real question how much of the rapid transformation of America has been marked by actual mobility in the sense of advancement by the individual through the ranks of society from one status to another and how much has been a mere change in the manner of life and standard of living of classes which retain pretty much the same relative position. The middle-class city dweller of today has a money income that would have connoted wealth to his frugal, landowning, farm-dwelling forebear of the nineteenth century, and his facilities for living make his forebear's life seem Spartan by comparison; but his standing in the community is no higher and is, in fact, considerably less independent. Improvements in the standard of living of society at large should not be confused with the achievement of separate social advancement by individuals.

But even allowing for this distinction, it bears repeating that America has had a greater measure of social equality and social mobility than any highly developed society in human history. In terms of geographical movement ("horizontal mobility," as it is sometimes called), it has been characteristically American for the individual to make his life in a place distant from his family home, which is to say that he achieves his own status instead of receiving one which is entailed upon him. In terms of economic and social ups and downs ("vertical mobility," so called) America has been the country where the cycle "from shirtsleeves to shirtsleeves" was three generations, which is to say that status has changed readily and rapidly.

In America, education has been more available to people with native ability; a professional and business opportunities have been more available to people with education; wealth has been more available to people who excelled in business and the professions; and social fortresses have yielded to the assaults of wealth more readily than in any other country. At every stage, the channels of mobility have been kept open. As for social distinctions, certainly they exist; but, whatever their power may be, social rank can seldom assert an open claim to deference in this country, and it usually makes at least a pretense of conformity to equalitarian ways. Certain conspicuous exceptions, such as the treatment of American Negroes, qualify all these assertions but do not invalidate them as generalizations.

Americans have attached immense value, of course, to this condition of equal opportunity. It has, they feel, enabled men and women in this country, more than anywhere else in the world, to find, develop, and exercise their best potentialities as human beings. Such opportunity has not only meant fulfilment for the individual; it has also been of great value to society: it has enabled the nation to make the optimum use of its human resources by recruiting talent from the whole body of the population and not merely from a limited class, and thus it has strengthened the arts, the sciences, the economic enterprise, and the government of the country.

Moreover, American society, as a society of abundance, especially needed men who would accept the challenge of mobility. Historically, as new lands, new forms of wealth, new opportunities, came into play, clamoring to be seized upon, America developed something of a compulsion to make use of them. The man best qualified for this role was the completely mobile man, moving freely from one locality to the next, from one economic position to another, or from one social level to levels above. The rapidity of economic change required a high degree of convertibility, of transmutability, in the economic elements which it employed, and the system of mobility imparted this necessary flexibility in the human resources which were needed. In a country where the entire environment was to be transformed with the least possible delay, a man who was not prepared to undergo personal transformation was hardly an asset. Hence mobility became not merely an optional privilege but almost a mandatory obligation, and the man who failed to meet this obligation had, to a certain extent, defaulted in his duty to society.

Because of these values and these compulsions, America not only practiced a full measure of mobility and social equality but also developed a creed of equality and articulated a myth to accompany the creed.

The myth of equality held that equality exists not merely as a potentiality in the nature of man but as a working actuality in the operation of American society—that advantages or handicaps are not really decisive and that every man is the architect of his own destiny. It asserted the existence in the United States of a classless society, where no one is better than anyone else and merit is the only recognized ground of distinction. Despite their patent implausibility, these ideas received and still retain a most tenacious hold. Americans are notoriously unresponsive to the concept of class warfare, and American workers, while fully alert to the protection of their economic interests, have never accepted identity as members of a working class in the way in which workers in England and other countries have. . . .

In the rearing of a child, it would be difficult to imagine any factors more vital than the distinction between a permissive and an authoritarian regime or more vital than the age at which economic responsibility is imposed. In both these matters the modern American child lives under a very different dispensation from children in the past. We commonly think of these changes as results of our more enlightened or progressive or humanitarian ideas. We may even think of them as results of developments in the specific field of child psychology, as if the changes were simply a matter of our understanding these matters better than our grandparents. But the fact is that the authoritarian discipline of the child, within the authoritarian family, was but an aspect of the authoritarian social system that was linked with the economy of scarcity. Such a regime could never have been significantly relaxed within the family so long as it remained diagnostic in the society. Nor could it have remained unmodified within the family, once society began to abandon it in other spheres.

Inevitably, the qualities which parents inculcate in a child will depend upon the roles which they occupy themselves. For the ordinary man the economy of scarcity has offered one role, as Simon N. Patten observed many years ago, and the economy of abundance has offered another. Abundance offers "work calling urgently for workmen"; scarcity found the "worker seeking humbly any kind of toil." As a suppliant to his superiors, the worker under scarcity accepted the principle of authority; he accepted his own subordination and the obligation to cultivate the qualities appropriate to his subordination, such as submissiveness, obedience, and deference. Such a man naturally transferred the principle of authority into his own family and, through this principle, instilled into his children the qualities appropriate to people of their kind—submissiveness, obedience, and deference. Many copybook maxims still exist to remind us of the firmness of childhood discipline, while the difference between European and American children—one of the most clearly recognizable of all national differences—serves to emphasize the extent to which Americans have now departed from this firmness.

This new and far more permissive attitude toward children has arisen, significantly, in an economy of abundance, where work has called urgently for the workman. In this situation, no longer a suppliant, the workman found submissiveness no longer a necessity and therefore no longer a virtue. The principle of authority lost some of its majesty, and he was less likely to regard it as the only true criterion of domestic order. In short, he ceased to impose it upon his children. Finding that the most valuable trait in himself was a capacity for independent decision and self-reliant conduct in dealing with the diverse opportunities which abundance offered him, he tended to encourage this quality in his children. The irresponsibility of childhood still called for a measure of authority on one side and obedience on the other, but this became a means to an end and not an end in itself. On the whole, permissive training, to develop independent ability, even though it involves a certain sacrifice of obedience and discipline, is the characteristic mode of child-rearing in the one country which most distinctively enjoys an economy of abundance. Here, in a concrete way, one finds something approaching proof for Gerth and Mills's suggestion that the relation of father and child may have its importance not as a primary factor but rather as a "replica of the power relations of society."

If scarcity required men to "seek humbly any kind of toil," it seldom permitted women to seek employment outside the home at all. Consequently, the woman was economically dependent upon, and, accordingly, subordinate to, her husband or her father. Her subordination reinforced the principle of authority within the home. But the same transition which altered the role of the male worker has altered her status as well, for abundance "calling urgently for workmen" makes no distinctions of gender, and, by extending economic independence to women, has enabled them to assume the role of partners rather than of subordinates within the family. Once the relation of voluntarism and equality is introduced between husband and wife, it is, of course, far more readily extended to the relation between parent and child.

If abundance has fostered a more permissive regime for the child, amid circumstances of democratic equality within the family, it has no less certainly altered the entire process of imposing economic responsibility upon the child, hence the process of preparing the child for such responsibility. In the economy of scarcity, as I have remarked above, society could not afford to support any substantial quota of nonproductive members. Consequently, the child went to work when he was as yet young. He attended primary school for a much shorter school year than the child of today; only a minority attended high school; and only the favored few attended college. Even during the brief years of schooling, the child worked, in the home, on the farm, or even in the factory. But today the economy of abundance can afford to maintain a substantial proportion of the population in nonproductive status, and it assigns this role, sometimes against their will, to its younger and its elder members. It protracts the years of schooling, and it defers responsibilities for an unusually long span. It even enforces laws setting minimal ages for leaving school, for going to work, for consenting to sexual intercourse, or for marrying. It extends the jurisdiction of juvenile courts to the eighteenth or the twentieth year of age.

Such exemption from economic responsibility might seem to imply a long and blissful youth free from strain for the child. But the delays in reaching economic maturity are not matched by comparable delays in other phases of growing up. On the contrary, there are many respects in which the child matures earlier. Physically, the child at the lower social level will actually arrive at adolescence a year or so younger than his counterpart a generation ago, because of improvement in standards of health and nutrition. Culturally, the child is made aware of the allurements of sex at an earlier age, partly by his familiarity with the movies, television, and popular magazines, and partly by the practice of "dating" in the early teens. By the standards of his peer group, he is encouraged to demand expensive and mature recreations, similar to those of adults, at a fairly early age. By reason of the desire of his parents that he should excel in the mobility race and give proof during his youth of the qualities which will make him a winner in later life, he is exposed to the stimuli of competition before he leaves the nursery. Thus there is a kind of imbalance between the postponement of responsibility and the quickening of social maturity which may have contributed to make American adolescence a more difficult age than human biology alone would cause it to be. Here, again, there are broad implications for the formation of character, and here, again, abundance is at work on both sides of the equation, for it contributes as much to the hastening of social maturity as it does to the prolongation of economic immaturity.

Some of these aspects of the rearing of children in the United States are as distinctively American, when compared with other countries, as any Yankee traits that have ever been attributed to the American people. In the multiplicity which always complicates social analysis, such aspects of child-rearing might be linked with a number of factors of American life. But one of the more evident and more significant links, it would seem certain, is with the factor of abundance. Such a tie is especially pertinent in this discussion, where the intention of the whole book has been to relate the study of character, as the historian would approach it, to the same subject as it is viewed by the behavioral scientist. In this chapter, especially, the attempt has been made to throw a bridge between the general historical force of economic abundance and the specific behavioral pattern of people's lives. Historical forces are too often considered only in their public and over-all effects, while private lives are interpreted without sufficient reference to the historical determinants which shape them. But no major force at work in society can possibly make itself felt at one of these levels without also having its impact at the other level. In view of this fact, the study of national character should not stand apart, as it has in the past, from the study of the process of character formation in the individual. In view of this fact, also, the effect of economic abundance is especially pertinent. For economic abundance is a factor whose presence and whose force may be clearly and precisely recognized in the most personal and intimate phases of the development of personality in the child. Yet, at the same time, the presence and the force of this factor are recognizable with equal certainty in the whole broad, general range of American experience, American ideals, and American insitutions. At both levels, it has exercised a pervasive influence in the shaping of the American character.

Chapter 4 THE NEW AMERICAN CHARACTER

*DAVID RIESMAN (1909-   ), a lawyer become
imaginative sociologist, is presently Henry Ford II
Professor of the Social Sciences at Harvard University. During the 1950's Riesman, who was influenced
by the writings of Thorstein Veblen, published* The
Lonely Crowd *and other influential books in which
he identified a new character type in contemporary
life, notably in American society. He termed this the
"other-directed person," who obtained his reference
points from the kaleidoscope of peers and the mass
media, in contrast to the older "inner-directed
person" who valued work and acted from internalized
motives and fixed moral principles. Riesman relates
this shift to a stage of incipient population decline.
Like David Potter in an earlier essay, he is attentive to
the social significance of permissive child rearing. He
also senses the plight of other-directed parents in
guiding their children and points to the problems of
authority in modern American society. Riesman
deals, too, with changing patterns involving liesure,
sex, the role of women, and the search for meaning.
These issues were new in the Eisenhower Era but have
become more urgent with passing years.*

. . . . If we wanted to cast our social character types into social class molds, we could say that inner-direction is the typical character of the "old" middle class—the banker, the tradesman, the small entrepreneur, the technically oriented engineer, etc.—while other-direction is becoming the typical character of the "new" middle class—the bureaucrat, the salaried employee in business, etc. Many of the economic factors associated with the recent growth of the "new" middle class are well known. They have been discussed by James Burnam, Colin Clark, Peter Drucker, and others. There is a decline in the numbers and in the proportion of the working population engaged in production and extraction—agriculture, heavy industry, heavy transport—and an increase in the numbers and the proportion engaged in white-collar work and the service trades.

David Riesman in collaboration with Reuel Denney and Nathan Glazer, *The Lonely Crowd: A Study of the Changing American Character* (New Haven: Yale University Press, 1950), pp. 21-23, 47-49, 153-157, 169-171. Reprinted by permission. Footnotes omitted.

Furthermore, societies in the phase of incipient decline (societies, that is, in which we expect other-directed types to come to the fore) are not only highly urbanized but have a high level of capital equipment and technological skill built up during the period of transitional growth. People who are literate, educated, and provided with the necessities of life by machine industry and agriculture, turn increasingly to the "tertiary" economic realm. The service industries prosper among the people as a whole and no longer only in court circles. Education, leisure, services, these go together with an increased consumption of words and images from the mass media of communications in societies that have moved into the incipient decline stage via the route of industrialization. Hence, while societies in the phase of transitional growth begin the process of distributing words from urban centers, the flow becomes a torrent in the societies of incipient population decline. This process, while modulated by profound national and class differences, connected with differences in literacy and loquacity, takes place everywhere in the industrialized lands. Increasingly, relations with the outer world and with oneself are mediated by the flow of mass communication. For the other-directed types political events are likewise experienced through a screen of words by which the events are habitually atomized and personalized—or pseudopersonalized. For the inner-directed person who remains still extant in this period the tendency is rather to systematize and moralize this flow of words.

These developments lead, for large numbers of people, to changes in paths to success and to the requirement of more "socialized" behavior both for success and for marital and personal adaptation. Connected with such changes are changes in the family and in child-rearing practices. In the smaller families of urban life, and with the spread of "permissive" child care to ever wider strata of the population, there is a relaxation of older patterns of discipline. Under these newer patterns the peer-group (the age- and class-graded group in a child's school and neighborhood) becomes much more important to the child, while the parents make him feel guilty not so much about violation of inner standards as about failure to be popular or otherwise to manage his relations with these other children. Moreover, the pressures of the school and the peer-group are reinforced and continued—in a manner whose inner paradoxes I shall discuss later—by the mass media: movies, radio, comics, and popular culture media generally. Under these conditions types of character emerge that we shall here term other-directed. To them much of the discussion in the ensuing chapters is devoted. *What is common to all other-directeds is that their contemporaries are the source of direction for the individual—either those known to him or those with whom he is indirectly acquainted, through friends and through the mass media. This source is of course "internalized" in the sense that dependence on it for guidance in life is implanted early. The goals toward which the other-directed person strives shift with that guidance: it is only the process of striving itself and the process of paying close attention to the signals from others that remain unaltered throughout life.* This mode of keeping in touch with others permits a close behavioral conformity, not through drill in behavior itself, as in the tradition-directed character, but rather through an exceptional sensitivity to the actions and wishes of others.

Of course, it matters very much who these "others" are: whether they are the individual's immediate circle or a "higher" circle or the anonymous voices of the mass media; whether the individual fears the hostility of chance acquaintances or only of those who "count." But his need for approval and direction from others—and contemporary others rather than ancestors—goes beyond the reasons that lead most people in any era to care very much what others think of them. While all people want and need to be liked by some of the people some of the time, it is only the modern other-directed types who make this their chief source of direction and chief area of sensitivity. . . .

Here again the new developments are most marked in the United States even though the rise of the new middle class is a phenomenon of other western countries as well. In 1947 C. Wright Mills of Columbia University obtained a number of intensive interviews with white-collar employees in and near New York: shopgirls, insurance salesmen, receptionists, and so on. Reading the reports of these interviews, I was struck by the extent of which these people, often coming from backgrounds where inner-direction prevailed, manifested other-directed patterns of behavior. Their work meant to them primarily getting along with people. They saw advancement—and, beyond that, happiness—in terms of improving their social skills. And they looked to their contemporaries for guidance not only as to how to do things but as to what things were worth doing. While we speak in this book primarily of the upper ranks of the middle class in the larger cities, both Mills's interviews and our own (in which we used some of the same questions developed by Mills) seemed to us to indicate that the other-directed character is widely distributed, at least in certain white-collar occupations of the lower middle class—where, indeed, other-direction is often more helpless, more overt, more submissive. Nor are such tendencies absent among young people from farm and factory families.

Under the new conditions of social and economic life parents who try, in inner-directed fashion, to compel the internalization of disciplined pursuit of clear goals run the risk of having their children styled clear out of the personality market. Gyroscopic direction is just not flexible enough for the rapid adaptations of personality that are required, precisely because there will be other competitors who do not have gyroscopes. Inhibited from presenting their children with sharply silhouetted images of self and society, parents in our era can only equip the child to do his best, whatever that may turn out to be. What is best is not in their control but in the hands of the school and peer-group that will help locate the child eventually in the hierarchy. But even these authorities speak vaguely; the clear principles of selection that once guided people of inner-directed character no longer apply. For example, social climbing itself may be called into public question at the same time that it is no longer so unequivocally desirable in terms of private wish. As recent *Fortune* surveys indicated, a safe and secure job may be preferred to a risky one involving high stakes. What is more, it is no longer clear which way *is* up even if one wants to rise, for with the growth of the new middle class the older, hierarchical patterns disintegrate, and it is not easy to compare ranks among the several sets of hierarchies that do exist. Does an army colonel "rank" the head of an international union? A physics professor, a bank vice-president? A commentator, the head of an oil company?

Increasingly in doubt as to how to bring up their children, parents turn to other contemporaries for advice; they also look to the mass media; and like the mother quoted at the outset of this chapter they turn, in effect, to the children themselves. They may, nevertheless, fasten on some inflexible scheme of child rearing and follow that. Yet they cannot help show their children, by their own anxiety, how little they depend on themselves and how much on others. Whatever they may seem to be teaching the child in terms of content, they are passing on to him their own contagious, highly diffuse anxiety. They reinforce this teaching by giving the child approval—and approving themselves because of the child— when he makes good.

To be sure, inner-directed parents also often were able to "love" only those children who made good in the outer world. But at least the canons of success were reasonably clear. The other-directed child, however, faces not only the requirement that he make good but also the problem of defining what making good means. He finds that both the definition and the evaluation of himself depend on the company he keeps: first, on his schoolmates and teachers; later, on peers and superiors. But perhaps the company one keeps is itself at fault? One can then shop for other preferred companies in the mass circulation media.

Approval itself, irrespective of content, becomes almost the only unequivocal good in this situation: one makes good when one is approved of. Thus all power, not merely some power, is in the hands of the actual or imaginary approving group, and the child learns from his parents' reactions to him that nothing in his character, no possession he owns, no inheritance of name or talent, no work he has done is valued for itself but only for its effect on others. Making good becomes almost equivalent to making friends, or at any rate the right kind of friends. "To him that hath approval, shall be given more approval." . . .

In the era depending on inner-direction sex might be inhibited, as in classes and areas affected strongly by the Reformation and Counter Reformation. Or its gratification might be taken for granted among men and within given limits, as in Italy, Spain, and the nonrespectable elements, such as the "riverbottom people," in every population. In both cases there was a certain simplification of sex, in the one instance by taboos, in the other by tradition. Economic or power problems, problems of mere existence or of "amounting to something," were uppermost; and sex was relegated to its "proper" time and place: night, the wife or whore, occasional rough speech, and daydreams. Only in the upper classes, precursors of modern other-directed types, did the making of love take precedence over the making of goods (allegedly so in France) and reach the status of a daytime agenda. In these circles sex was almost totally separated from reproduction.

This separation, when it goes beyond the upper class and spreads over almost the whole society, is a sign that a society, through birth control and all that it implies, has entered the population phase of incipient decline by the route of industrialization. In this phase there is not only a growth of leisure, but work itself becomes both less interesting and less demanding for many; increased supervision and subdivision of tasks routinize the industrial process even beyond what was accomplished in the phase of transitional growth of population. More than before, as job-mindedness declines, sex permeates the daytime as well as the playtime consciousness. It is viewed as a consumption good not only by the old leisure classes but by the modern leisure masses.

The other-directed person, who suffers from low responsiveness, may pursue what looks like a "cult of effortlessness" in many spheres of life. He may welcome the routinization of his economic role and of his domestic life; the auto companies may tempt him by self-opening windows and self-shifting gears; he may withdraw all emotion from politics. Yet he cannot handle his sex life in this way. Though there is tremendous insecurity about *how* the game of sex should be played, there is little doubt as to *whether* it should be played or not. Even when we are consciously bored with sex, we must still obey its drive. Sex, therefore, provides a kind of defense against the threat of total apathy. This is one of the reasons why so much excitement is channeled into sex by the other-directed person. He looks to it for reassurance that he is alive. The inner-directed person, driven by his internal gyroscope and oriented toward the production problems of the outer world, did not need this evidence. Moreover, his relatively unemancipated wife and socially inferior mistresses could not seriously challenge the quality of his sexual performance.

While the inner-directed acquisitive consumer could pursue the ever receding frontiers of material acquisition, these frontiers have lost much of their lure for the other-directed person. As we saw in Chapter III, the latter begins as a very young child to know his way around among available consumption goods. He travels widely, to camp or with his family. He knows that the rich man's car is only marginally, if at all, different from his own—a matter at best of a few additional horsepower. He knows anyway that next year's model will be better than this year's. Even if he has not been there, he knows what the night clubs are like; and he has seen television. Whereas the deprived inner-directed person often lusted for possessions as a goal whose glamour a wealthy adulthood could not dim, the other-directed person can scarcely conceive of a consumption good that can maintain for any length of time undisputed dominance over his imagination. Except perhaps sex.

For the making and consumption of love, despite all the efforts of the mass media, do remain hidden from public view. If someone else has a new Cadillac, the other-directed person knows what that is, and that he can duplicate the experience, more or less. But if someone else has a new lover, he cannot know what that means. Cadillacs have been democratized. So has sexual glamour, to a degree: without the mass production of good-looking, well-groomed youth, the American pattern of sexual competition could not exist. But there is a difference between Cadillacs and sexual partners in the degree of mystery. And with the loss of submergence of moral change and inhibitions, but not completely of a certain unconscious innocence, the other-directed person has no defenses against his own envy. He is not ambitious to break the quantitative records of the acquisitive sex consumers like Don Juan, but he does not want to miss, day in day out, the qualities of experience he tells himself the others are having.

In a way this development is paradoxical. For while cookbooks have become more glamorous with the era of other-direction, sex books have become less so. The older marriage manuals, such as that of Van der Velde (still popular, however), breathe an ecstatic tone; they are travelogues of the joy of love. The newer ones, including some high school sex manuals, are matter of fact, toneless, and hygienic— Boston Cooking School style. Nevertheless, much as young people may appear to take sex in stride along with their vitamins, it remains an area of competition and a locus of the search, never completely suppressed, for meaning and emotional response in life. The other-directed person looks to sex not for display but for a test of his or her ability to attract, his or her place in the "rating-dating" scale—and beyond that, in order to experience life and love.

One reason for the change is that women are no longer objects for the acquisitive consumer but are peer-groupers themselves. Freed by technology from many household tasks, given by technology many "aids to romance," millions of women have become pioneers, with men, on the frontier of sex. As they become knowing consumers, the anxiety of men lest they fail to satisfy the women also grows—but at the same time this is another test that attracts men who, in their character, want to be judged by others. The very ability of women to respond in a way that only courtesans were supposed to in an earlier age means, moreover, that qualitative differences of sex experience—the impenetrable mystery—can be sought for night after night, and not only in periodic visits to a mistress or brothel. Whereas the pattern of an earlier era was often to make fun of sex, whether on the level of the music hall or of Balzac's *Droll Stories*, sex today carries too much psychic freight to be really funny for the other-directed person. By a disguised asceticism it becomes at the same time too anxious a business and too sacred an illusion. Popular culture, as Everett Hughes has pointed out, increasingly plays sex for excitement, not for a laugh.

The work of Kinsey, valuable as it is, does not provide us with data concerning qualitative shifts of the sort described—shifts confined in any case to a minority of the population. But it makes sense to suppose that the inner-directed person, for whom sex is a variation from his workaday role—a variation modified no doubt by sublimations, repressions, and displacements—will regard sex differently from the other-directed person, for whom life generally is geared to interpersonal relations in both work and leisure and for whom meaning and excitement is found in "taking the role of the other."

This anxious competitiveness in the realm of sex has very little in common with older patterns of social climbing. To be sure, women still use sex as a means to status in spheres controlled by men. But they can do this chiefly in industries that are still competitive in the premonopolistic patterns. Thus until recently the theater and the movies were controlled by *novi homines* who remind us of those early nineteenth-century British mill owners who, before the Factory Acts, relied on their mills as a harem. And Warner, Havighurst, and Loeb in *Who Shall be Educated?* describe how women schoolteachers may still cabin-date their way in the relatively unbureaucratized hierarchies of local school systems. These, however, are exceptional cases; consumption habits in food and sex have, for most consumers, only the most peripheral connections with social mobility.

A particularly striking illustration of the use of leisure by the other-directed person for whom means have become ends is the cult of sun tanning. Marginal differentiation by means of bodily adornment (of which sun tanning is of course but one style) we know to be characteristic of all cultures. Yet there is a difference between contemporary American concern for body image and the patterns to be found elsewhere. For one thing, competition in dress, war paint, or tattooing is definitely related in most cultures to other "external" conventions such as one's status in the social hierarchy or one's role in the economy. But competition in body shape and color as it appears so intensely in America is not related to economic or social advance and only marginally even to sexual conquest. Color competition is an end in itself, not a means to any other end nor an insignia of one's achievements. In summer and even in winter both men and women enter a beauty contest in which they can appraise their personalities and compare nuances in shade and hue of epiderm. Their taste buds, tastes, body image and skin, their "pep," "vitality," and intellectual and sensuous qualities, are not exploited as avenues of ascent in a well-defined hierarchy. Instead, they are opened to inspection and introspection by a desire to share in the leisure agendas of the adult self-exploiting peer-group. . . .

So far, in these illustrations, we have seen little that would correspond to the unambiguous escapes of the inner-directed. Rather, we have seen popular culture used, often quite desperately, for training in consumer orientation and group adjustment. Despite appearances the other-directed person seems often unable to get away from himself or to waste time with any gestures of abundance or abandon. (Of course, if we compared patterns of alcoholic escape, we might come up with somewhat different results.)

The inner-directed person, if influenced by Protestantism, is of course also unable to waste time. The mobile youth from the lower classes shows his commitment to inner-direction by cutting himself off from hard-drinking, horse-play-in-dulging pals: he continues the production of an inner-directed character through practicing a kind of mental bookkeeping by which the demons of Waste and Sloth are ruthlessly driven out. Such a person has little leisure, unless he can justify it as self-improving, and a life that has never an idle moment must have many a tense one. On the face of it the other-directed person is no puritan; he seems much less preoccupied with waste. But an attenuated puritanism survives in his exploitation of his leisure. He may say, when he takes a vacation or stretches a weekend, "I owe it to myself"—but the self in question is viewed like a car or house whose upkeep must be carefully maintained for resale purposes. The other-directed person has no clear core of self to escape from; no clear line between production and consumption; between adjusting to the group and serving private interests; between work and play.

One interesting index of this is the decline of evening dress, especially among men, and conversely, the invasion of the office by sport clothes. This looks like an offshoot of the cult of effortlessness, and of course men say "it's too much trouble" in explaining why they don't change for dinner or the evening. But the answer lies rather in the fact that men today simply do not know how to change roles, let alone mark the change by proper costuming. Another reason may be the fear of being thought high-hat; one can wear gaudy shirts but not stiff ones. Thus the sport shirt and casual dress show that one is a good fellow not only on the golf course or on vacation but in the office and at dinner too.

Women are still permitted-required to dress for the evening, a sign, perhaps, of their laggard response to changing modes. (Similarly, one would expect to find tuxedos more frequently worn among the Negro than among the white middle classes.) Women are more involved than men in the dying patterns of conspicuous consumption. However, they probably make more of an actual shift from house-work and babies to dinner party than many men do, who exchange office gossip both at work and play: moreover, they really like the shift, dragging the men, who would just as soon be in the office, along with them. I have observed that women's shop talk of children and domestic matters is often—though certainly not always! —conducted with more skill, interest, and realism than that of men since the change of role refreshes both work and play.

What is it that drives men who have been surrounded with people and their problems on the day shift to seek often exactly the same company (or its reflection in popular culture) on the night shift? Perhaps in part it is the terror of loneliness that the gangster movies symbolize. But certainly it makes for strain. Though popular culture on one level "fills in" between people so as to avoid any demand for conversational or sexual gambits, on another level the popular-culture perform-ance is not simply a way of killing time: in the peer-group situation, it makes a demand that it be appraised. The other-directed girl who goes in company to the movies need not talk to the others during the picture but is sometimes faced with the problem: should she cry at the sad places or not? What is the proper reaction, the sophisticated line about what is going on? Observing movie audiences coming out of a "little" or "art" theater, it is sometimes apparent that people feel they ought to react, but how?

As against this, the inner-directed person, reading a book alone, is less aware of the others looking on; moreover, he has time to return at his own pace from being transported by his reading—to return and put on whatever mask he cares to. The poker game in the back room, with its praise of masks, fits his habituation to social distance, even loneliness. His successor, dreading loneliness, tries to assuage it not only in his crowd but in a song like "Night and Day."

Popular culture, then, is used as an indirect recourse to people. When I asked young people in interviews how they would feel if for some reason the radio should be shut off, quite a few were frightened at the prospect. They asked, "Is the government planning to do that to us?" One veteran of the Pacific campaign, who had spent two years in Korea, said he had once been at a summer place in Wisconsin where for two weeks there had been no radio. He said he couldn't stand it; nothing in the army, where he had the Armed Forces Network, was so bad. Without the noise of the radio, it seems, people feel as if their own receptors are dead. And indeed they have used the noise of the others to deaden the noise of the self....

Chapter 5   CHANGING LIFE STYLES AND THE VOGUE OF ADJUSTMENT

RUSSELL LYNES, JR. (1910-   ), managing editor of Harper's from 1947 to 1967 and at present a contributing editor of that magazine, is an able cultural historian. Lynes, who also has written several witty books on postwar mores and manners, including Highbrow, Lowbrow, Middlebrow *(1949) and* Snobs *(1950), turned his attention to the new prosperity with* A Surfeit of Honey *(1953). After discussing changing family roles and the increasing informality of American life, Lynes comments on the decline among students of the ideal of success and the vogue of well-roundedness and adjustment. Lynes, who reveals Riesman's influence, also hints at a social explanation of the middle-road political views of the Eisenhower Era.*

. . . . Look what has happened to the innocent, peace-loving husband in this best of all possible worlds.

Recently a friend of mine told me of a telephone conversation he had had with a young man who is a neighbor of his.

"I wish I could," the young man said. "There's nothing I'd like better, but I'm up to my elbows in diapers." The young neighbor is the father of two, the more recent one very recent indeed. My friend had asked him to play tennis, and he reported to me that, when he hung up, his feeling was not one of surprise or pity; it was one of guilt.

"I didn't say to myself, 'The poor hen-pecked fellow'," he told me with some shock in his voice. "I just said to myself, 'Well, I guess I ought to be doing my household chores too.' What kind of reaction do you call that?"

The narrow-gauge train of thought that this conversation set in motion in my mind led me to speculate about the nature of husbands and the recent changes in their behavior around the house. How did it happen that my friend's friend was diapering and that my friend thought he should be dusting and waxing? What would my father have thought of such behavior? I laughed out loud.

Bernard DeVoto once remarked to a colleague of mine, "What every career woman needs is a good wife." When he made this observation a number of years ago, the atmosphere of marriage was somewhat different from the atmosphere today. Only a woman with a career was then expected to have someone else assume the burdens of the household for her. It is only quite recently that (in cities and suburbs especially) every woman, regardless of her notions about a career, has adopted a different attitude. Now she takes it for granted that, when she marries, she is bound to get, almost as though it were a package deal, a husband who is also a part-time wife.

To call him a wife is, perhaps, to put it too bluntly. He is rather more servant than wife, though the distinction is sometimes a fine one. With a few interesting exceptions, the roles of the husband and wife are becoming less and less sharply differentiated. Whereas it was once a question of "Who wears the pants in this family?" it is now a matter of pants all around, and the children are as likely to cling to Father's apron strings as Mother's. You may have noticed that, in recent years, women have come to refer to their husbands more and more often as their "mates"—a sexually indeterminate word and one that implies equality. Man, once known as "the head of the family," is now partner in the family firm, part-time man, part-time mother and part-time maid. He is the chief cook and bottle washer; the chauffeur, the gardener, and the houseboy; the maid, the laundress, and the charwoman. . . .

But the scarcity of servants and the flood of gadgets that could be bought on time payments tell only part of the story of man's new captivity by women. World War II tore many families apart, and when they were put back together again, a strange new domestic pattern emerged that was quite unlike anything Americans had ever seen before. Millions of veterans went to college or to professional or trade schools on the GI bill. Many of these men were married and had small children, and in order to make ends meet, young wives went out and got jobs. Father, who had learned to make beds, darn socks, and police up in the Army, was left with his books and his babies and his broom. He became not only a wife but a mother, and he was grateful for the chance to re-establish his life this way, hopeful that the day would come when he might take off his apron and get out in the world. Those were the days when men used to gather in the self-service laundry and swap stories as they once had in the corner bar.

With our usual adaptability we have taken the shortage of servants, the influx of gadgets, the domestic skills that men learned as soldiers, the new role of women and docility of men, and out of them have created a new mode of life. Our image of the ideal family has changed from one in which Father laid down the law while Mother made the wheels go round to something far more like a team roughly the size and character of a basketball team. The ball is passed from hand to hand and the responsibility is shared by everybody.

At the same time, we have become devoted to what Frederick Lewis Allen called "the cult of informality." With nobody to cook and serve dinner at a given hour, we eat when we please and where we please—in the living room, in the back yard, in the kitchen. Not so long ago, most families, whether they could afford servants or not, used to observe many of the same formalities observed in families who were elaborately waited on. Now the families who can still afford servants affect many of the informalities of those who have none. The tables, you might say, have been turned into trays on the lap, the sit-down dinner has become a feast of squat-and-scramble. Some member of the family is always on his feet fetching something from the kitchen. Families, like toasters, have become pop-up, and Father no longer sits and is waited on. . . .

Not long ago I was asked by the editors of *Mademoiselle* magazine to shuffle through a stack of questionnaires that they had sent to several hundred young women in their last years of college and several hundred others who had recently graduated. The questionnaires were intended to pry out of these young women their notions of success—in college, in jobs, in marriage. Unlike many questionnaires that I have examined these seemed to me agreeably civilized both in the questions asked and in the ways in which they were answered.

Some of the young ladies were wistful, some defiant; some were puzzled, quizzical, romantic, and some, but only a few, had a glint of hard ambition. A few were blasé or smug. But all of them seemed to be frank. "Private faces in public places," W. H. Auden wrote, "are wiser and nicer than public faces in private places." The private faces that looked up at me from the questionnaires were, many of them, wise and nice, but I scarcely recognized them. The meaning of personal success, not very long ago thought to be "the attainment of wealth, fame, etc." (Webster's) had changed. The look in the eyes seemed different from the look I was used to seeing in the young. Wealth and fame, it would seem, are not worth the bother and the sacrifice; the aim has become well-roundedness.

Success has become a matter of neither impinging too insistently on the world nor letting the world impinge any more than is essential on one's self. The dream is of comfort and not excitement, of security and not prominence, of developing as many of one's potentialities as possible in a modest way without letting any one of them run away with the others. A job is a way of meeting "interesting people," of keeping amused, but it must not be all-absorbing. "I think definitely that a job should not consume your life," wrote a girl from the University of Texas. "It should be one in which you are interested and which enables you to lead a well-rounded life." Another girl, from the University of Wisconsin, echoed this: she said that she was interested in a job, "but only to the extent that it wouldn't interfere with a well-rounded social life."

The devotion to well-roundedness appears to go further than just ambition for oneself. It applies equally to ambition for one's husband. Few of the private faces seemed interested in marrying a man determined to get to the top of his profession, who by hard and persistent work would push back the frontiers of his chosen field. They were thinking of his happiness and of his health, and they cast both in the setting of relaxed weekends—the picture of thoroughly barbecued bliss. "I want my husband to be ambitious but not dangerously so," wrote one college girl, and another said, "I don't want him to have such a high executive position that it would ruin his health or personal relationships with his friends or family." Throughout the answers there was a constant identification of work and achievement with ruined health, lost friends, unhappiness. It was associated with trampling on other people who are also on the ladder, with having no time for the children and working incessantly over weekends. "The college girl's picture of a Successful Person," commented one of the young editors of *Mademoiselle* who had spent a good deal of time over the questionnaires, "seems to be a combination of a bore, a bastard, and a battered-and-broken adventurer."

And money? Money is all right so long as you can buy happiness with it. A great deal of money, young women believe, can only be acquired at the sacrifice of virtue, sincerity, children, principles, and well-roundedness. "Just enough to get along comfortably," seems to be the goal, though the meaning of *comfortably* varied considerably from answer to answer. Most of all they want their husbands to be happy in their jobs, and not to break their necks or their hearts trying to get rich. "No job," wrote one girl, "should encroach on relaxing time." As you might expect, the young wives who answered the questionnaire that was sent them took a more lively interest than the college girls in the quantity as well as the quality of their husbands' pay checks.

The family is, of course, the ultimate measure of success—its solidarity, its community of interest, the well-being of the children. In this money plays a secondary role; it is time that matters—time for the husband and wife to putter together, to play with the children (three or four of them), to have neighbors in (nobody wants to entertain "business friends" if she can help it), and to indulge in what are known as "outside interests." The goal for marriage, like the goal in college, seemed to be characterized by a desire not for Phi Beta Kappa but an "all around good average." The key word is "adjustment" and the place is "to one's environment." Adjustment to one's environment is, I believe, the opposite of the conquest of it.

But these are generalities. Specifically, adjustment means a series of compromises between one's interests and one's ideal of the good life; environment means a good deal more than just place. First of all, environment means the family, and adjustment to it means marshaling all of one's other interests to making the family a success. It means supporting the careeer that your husband has chosen with enthusiasm tempered with sweet reasonableness, lest he overwork or overworry. It means seeing that one's children are given every opportunity for healthy and well-adjusted (there's that word again) lives. But environment also includes the world of the mind, and the concept of well-roundedness insists on the maintenance and development of one's intellectual interests. There must be time for reading, for concerts, for active participation in local educational and political matters. One should be "well-informed"; that is, one should be able to discuss international affairs with the same confidence that one discusses gardening, baseball, or Bartok.

The good, well-rounded life seems to be lived as much out of doors as in, for it is assumed that all men would rather be on the golf course, in the garden, on hikes and picnics, or in boats than anywhere else. This assumption is fortified by the belief that whatever interests a husband must also interest his wife and she must participate with the fullness of her heart, limbs, and mind. It seems as though life were to be lived on the college elective system with a major in homemaking and a minor in physical education. The life of the mind must be cultivated, but its activities are somewhat like those necessary but peripheral courses elected to complete the essential credits for a degree in well-rounded living.

To ignore the electives is to be a failure; it is to fall short of the ideal of success. How can you get along with all sorts of people (one of the primary qualities of being well balanced) unless you are alert and well informed and yet free of the lopsidedness so often associated with overconcentration? It is a life, obviously, that to be lived successfully has to be lived furiously in order to get everything in, and yet its essential quality is that of seeming relaxed and ready for anything. Wife, mother, pal; well read, well adjusted; tasteful, tactful, tolerant; active, patient, intelligent. And a lady besides? How does anyone have time to be well rounded?

If this is the success the young women of today are pursuing, they are embarked on careers of sweat and toil. While they are reading they will be worried about not being on the tennis court or at a PTA meeting, and while they are indulging their own predilections, they will be looking over their shoulders to see whether their taste manages at the same time to be personal and yet uneccentric. They must be concerned with expressing themselves without overstating their case; they must be creative without offending anyone—which, let it be said, is all but impossible. It is very likely to be the well rounded who are most offended.

Is there, do you suppose, any real risk of developing a criterion of success that is based on well-roundedness? A great many well-rounded young women summons up for me a large bunch of hothouse grapes—lovely to look at, plump, smooth, carefully protected from the crankiness of weather, and tasteless. Pebbles in a stream are also well-rounded; so are the vowels in the mouth of an elocution teacher. What is the likeness of the well-rounded male, the mate desired by the well-rounded female?

First of all he is affable, friendly, trustworthy and he tries to be all things to all people. He gets on easily with everybody, everybody, that is, who is also well rounded and even with a few who are not. He is conservative in his tastes for furniture, foods, entertainments, and women. He is conscientious, does his duty by his community and, when called upon, by his country. He never gets caught off balance (neither, incidentally, does a ball, which is also well-rounded), and he changes his mind slowly because he likes to see all sides of a problem. He is a man whose principles are not easily shaken, though he knows how to give a little here and take a little there; he recognizes that compromise is not without virtue if it is used for virtuous ends. He prefers the *status quo*, but he does not deny the processes of evolution. This tends to make him conservative in his political opinions, but he is not a reactionary. He is a middle-of-the-roader. He is a natural do-gooder within the realm of his convenience and of what he expects the opinion of his circle of friends to be. He is not, however, going to risk his position in the community by espousing an unpopular point of view. He pushes no frontiers back. He does not get "burned up" about anything, except, possibly, those things that threaten his position in the pyramid of society in which he lives or that might endanger his property values or the well-being of his family.

Someday I should like to meet the well-rounded man I have just described. He must be a rare and remarkable specimen. I doubt if he exists at all; he is merely a literary figment, the kind of man one discovers only by trying to strike an average from the answers to a questionnaire. He is not an individual; he is just a generality. He is a statistical meatball, the lean and the fat all ground together.

But there is evidence that the meatball is not unrelated to reality. David Riesman in an article in *The American Scholar* told of a study of Princeton seniors that had been made by *Time* magazine. Interviewers had asked the students what they thought their lives would be like in fifteen years. "No life in the ulcer belt for me," one of the young men said, and another said, "Why struggle on my own when I can enjoy the big psychological income of being a member of a big outfit?" The theme of well-roundedness emerges as clearly from the Princeton seniors as it did from the *Mademoiselle* girls. One young man who plans to be a lawyer said (and Mr. Riesman after some initial doubt decided that the young man wasn't trying to pull the interviewer's leg): "I'll belong to all the associations you can think of—Elks, VFWs, Boy Scouts and Boys' Clubs, YMCA, American Legion, etc. It will keep me away from home a lot. But my wife won't mind. She'll be vivacious and easy with people. And she will belong to everything in sight too—especially the League of Women Voters. I won't marry her until I'm twenty-eight, and so when I'm thirty-six we will have only two of the four children I hope for eventually. We'll be living in an upper middle class home costing about $20,000 by then, in a suburban fringe. . . .We'll have two Fords or Chevvies when I'm thirty-six, so we can both keep the busy schedule we'll have. But in addition to this public social life, we'll have private friends who don't even live around Toledo—friends with whom we can be completely natural and relaxed. That's where Princeton friends will be very important."

Mr. Riesman, who doesn't take the results of the *Time* survey too seriously, says of the young men: "The career they want is the good life, for which their corporation or profession serves as the good provider. These men already know they won't be president—they wouldn't want the job with its unpredictable demands, it presumptive big city locale, its disruption of family and recreational life."

The temptation to make a generation fit such a formula leads to alarm and distrust on the part of those who do not belong to it and disgust and boredom on the part of those who do. But this brief composite portrait of a generation's ideas of success is not entirely without validity, and if it seems to be without any very sharp edges we must remember that generations are also without edges; they are not compartments; they are merely what we mark off for the sake of convenience on a continuous line. . . .

Part Two THE DEBATE OVER CONSENSUS: CORPORATE STYLES AND PLURALISTIC POLITICS

Chapter 6 THE TRANSFORMED CORPORATION

In the following essay, first given as a lecture at Barnard College in 1953 and reprinted in Individualism Reconsidered *(1954),* DAVID RIESMAN *deftly probes new American attitudes toward work, risk-taking, consumption, the family, and human relations in business. Reflecting the intellectual outlook on America in the 1950's identified with "consensus," he suggests that college-educated professional managers were creating congenial corporate institutions that were a far cry from the horrors of the past and altogether suitable for contemporary life. He accordingly praises corporate "conspicuous production" as expressed in elegant buildings such as Lever House. Riesman correctly sensed that corporations had found an impressive and appropriate architecture, but he could not then see that the curtained-wall buildings of glass and steel might become rigid formulas leading to endless and sometimes tasteless repetition.*

. . . . An illustration of the slow way in which cultural definitions change lies in the fact that, as Americans have sloughed off to a considerable extent the Puritan's exalted valuations of work, we have nevertheless not on the whole sought jobs that would provide a maximum of income with a minimum of work. Rather, what has happened is that our aims have become more complex: we now seek "the right kind" of work, including the right blend of leisure with work and inside work. For instance, a recent series of articles in *Fortune* indicates that we are witnessing the death of our salesmen in general: companies are finding it more and more difficult to recruit salesmen, even or especially when they work on a commission basis. The

David Riesman, "New Standards for Old: From Conspicuous Consumption to Conspicuous Production," pp. 151-163. Reprinted with permission of MacMillan Publishing Co., Inc. from *Selected Essays from Individualism Reconsidered* by David Riesman. Copyright 1954 by The Free Press of Glencoe.

old-fashioned salesman sets his own pace; he had a great deal of leisure, and, if he was good and business was good, he could make money. But today such opportunities seem often to go begging, and corporations engage in all kinds of semantic niceties, such as redefining sales jobs as sales engineering to get around the problem; they try to replace direct selling by advertising, and by using the retail store as the point-of-sale as in the Supermarket. College graduates today want jobs in personnel work or other "service" occupations, rather than in the exposed and isolated position of the salesman. For one thing, their wives make more demands of them than Willy's wife did: they want them home, and free of ulcers—and these new-style wives are more help to their men than the neutral misery of Mrs. Loman was any comfort to Willy. In the old days, Biff might have become a salesman without afterthought, but his ambitions are confused by some of the newer currents.*

One reason for this is that young people seem to be increasingly choosing the role of an employee in a large organization, with pensions and perquisites, rather than the chance to make a quick killing by commission selling or other risky and entrepreneurial jobs. One company reported to *Fortune* that they now look for salesmen among Greeks—an ethnic group not yet acculturated to the newer American values; another, that they do their recruiting for sales in Texas and Oklahoma— states where also old-fashioned crazy millionaires can be still found. Sometimes people refer to high income taxes as a determining factor, but I think taxes, though certainly an element, are frequently used as rationalizations by men who don't want to take risks. Taxes are simply part of the managerial climate in which enterprise is now carried on, in which innovation is entrusted to a research and development staff trained at the Columbia School of Industrial Management and the Harvard Business School—men who take courses which deal with human relations in order that they will be able to get along with their colleagues in the office, or at least to discuss problems of human relations at American Management Association meetings.

And this leads me to a further reflection on *Death of a Salesman*. You will remember the terrible scene in which Howard Wagner fires Willy, while listening to an idiotic recording. Some of my colleagues at Chicago have recently been studying retirement practices and find that one reason many companies have a firm rule compelling retirement at, let us say, 65 is that people today are too soft-hearted to fire other people. At one large steel company, a number of older men have jobs which are make-work because no one can bring himself to discharge them. A retirement rule locates the responsibility elsewhere, makes it impersonal. This is true of the retirement regulations in universities also. Indeed, wherever I have observed such matters—in business, in government, in academic life—I have noticed the lengths to which people will go before firing somebody. Howard Wagners are

---

*Riesman refers to Willy Loman, a pathetic figure in the currently popular play by Arthur Miller, *Death of a Salesman*. Biff is Willy's son.

hard to come by. (You will notice that I am criticizing the play on the basis of a sociological estimate, but I must say that the play invites such criticism by its own effort at documentary realism.)

So far, I have spoken as if fear of risk was the chief factor in the actual dearth of entrepreneurs and of salesmen in the American economy at present. But there is also a growing desire to be serviceable to others—this is one reason for the current high prestige of the medical profession. The attraction of personnel work for many college graduates rests on their urge to work *with* people (the fact is, they more often work with files—but that is in a way beside the point) rather than, as they interpret selling, *against* people. People want to be part of a team, part of a group. Work is done in groups, research is done in groups. It is this security which is often more important than pension plans. (I am discussing at such length the problem of work and the salesman today, because in order to see clearly the changes in the standards for judging consumption, we have to see how work itself has changed. For work and play seem to be fundamental dualities in culture, like day and night, male and female, parent and child, self and not-self.)

It may be that the changes I have been discussing are partly kept from clearer view by the American belief that men must be tough, not soft and sentimental; thus, we tend to conceal from ourselves as well as from others our conciliatory attitudes, our moods of fearing success and display, our sensitivity to envy. And so we continue to talk about free enterprise, about getting ahead—about all the older values which the Loman family, in its several ways, has taken so literally. But often this talk is big talk, or whistling to keep up our courage. . . .

By the same evidence, we may conclude that there *have* been changes, very profound ones, although their origins can be traced back to an earlier day. Values once confined to a small elite group, or to an elite place within the hearts of many people—a kind of Sunday rather than weekday place—have now become much more widespread. For example, we can see this in attitudes towards conspicuous consumption. Veblen noticed in his book on the leisure class, published in 1899, that some small groups among the very rich were learning to be offended by conspicuous display, they were going in for "natural-looking" estates, "natural-looking" contrivances, and presumably "natural-looking" dress, too. He realized that when a leisure class gets large enough, and sufficiently in touch with itself, it can depart from grossly vulgar display—it can whisper rather than shout. And he saw how renewed attitudes of "workmanship," as against the earlier "wastemanship" at the top of the social pyramid, could spread downwards, as more people gained leisure, and as more came in contact with leisure class values.

Yet even he, perhaps because of his farm origin and midwest experience, did not see fully the extent of which nonconspicuous nonconsumption (or, as one of my friends more appropriately terms it, "conspicuous under-consumption") was already a powerful American pattern. He seems to have escaped contact with Boston

Unitarians or Philadelphia Quakers whose display was much more veiled. Although in Henry Adams' novel, *Democracy*, we are treated to an inauguration ball more gaudy than the un-top-hatted one of a few weeks ago [January, 1953], when we read Henry James's *The Bostonians*, which appeared in 1876, we are confronted with wealthy young women who were plain of dress and disdainful of display. For them, good intangible causes took the place of good commodities.

I should add, in fairness to Veblen, that he saw some of this. But he largely overlooked the possibility that these attitudes were being shaped by intellectual as well as by merely technological currents. Thus it would not have occurred to him that his own books would influence people's attitudes towards consumption, that he would be the godfather of the consumers' movement—that, indeed, a whole series of books, including his own and coming right down to Marquand's novels or *Death of a Salesman*, have helped inter certain American values with irony and sarcasm. For him, as for Marx, men always conform eventually to economic necessity, not to cultural or ideological necessity.

Nevertheless, Veblen's *Theory of the Leisure Class* fitted not too badly the American scene from the gay 90s to the not quite so gay 20s. The hero in the novel *Jefferson Selleck* who suffers agonies on his wedding night because he is of lower social origin than his bride; the drama of *The Great Gatsby*, and the miseries of Charlie Gray in *Point of No Return* and of Mary Monahan and her intimidated Beacon Street lover in the *Late George Apley*, are so many testimonies to the Veblenian cruelties of the American status system, with its unmerry emulative chase. And yet the last novels I mentioned are testimony also to a newer note in American life and literature, that of the failure of success, rather than, as in *Death of a Salesman*, the failure of failure.

It has, I believe, been the bounteousness of modern industry, especially in America, which has done more than almost anything else to make conspicuous consumption obsolete here. It would go much too far to say that consumption bores us, but it no longer has the old self-evident quality; it no longer furnishes our lives with a kind of simple structure or chronology of motives, as it did for William Randolph Hearst, for instance. To collect objects in Hearst's manner required a certain confidence, even arrogance, a certain imperviousness to ridicule and criticism. Hearst's "whim of iron" appears to be a thing of the past.

It is not only or primarily, however, that our interest in goods has been drowned by the boundless cornucopia of goods, by analogy with Engel's law that food consumption declines proportionately as income rises. The same expansion of the economy has created new fortunes much faster than their possessors could possibly be tutored by the old rich in the proper consumption values of the latter. No mere "400" located in a single city can any longer dictate appropriate leisure-class behavior in terms of what estates, houses, furniture, and so on to collect. The absence of titles in America, and of many old-family names equivalent to titles (judging by names, many Negroes and onetime Kabotskys belong to some of the best families), also makes such hegemony very difficult—indeed, from the point of view of an Italian count (unfamiliar with American distinctions even in the days of Daisy Miller), a Dallas oil heiress in seven figures and Neiman-Marcus clothes may be preferable to a Saltonstall in six figures and Jordon Marsh clothes. In this situation, the more established wealth and its auxiliary leaders of high taste have sought to fight back, not by a futile outspending, but by a conspicuous underspending. A Hearst has been ridiculed, not only for poor taste in *what* he bought, but *that* he bought in such quantity.

No doubt, universal education—itself part of our bonanza of good fortune—has exposed many people, who later have come into means, to tasteful critiques of working-class extravagance. The mass media, too, carry along with the prodigality of their advertising the relative emaciation of their judgments on expenditure: the *Vogue* style of restrained elegance is made an accessible model for millions. However, the movement of style has not only been from the top down—and how could it be when people can't tell, for reasons already indicated, where the top is? A relaxation of standards has spread upwards: the new rich gentleman needs no longer to struggle into a dress suit to hear Mary Garden at the Opera House, nor need he learn to ride to hounds or to send his sons to Groton or St. Marks. All he has to learn to do—and this, as Robert L. Steiner and Joseph Weiss point out in "Veblen Revised in the Light of Counter-Snobbery," is not easy for him—is to mute the wish for wild and gaudy spending that he learned as a lower-class lad, the very wish that may have helped propel him into the millionaire ranks. Frictions on this score are indicated by the concern of the Cadillac people with the consequences for their older clients of the fact that the Cadillac (rather than, as some years ago, the Buick) has become "the" car for well-off Negroes.

Today, men of wealth, fearful of making a wrong move, harried not only by taxes but by public relations and their own misgivings, are apt to give over the now-dreaded responsibilities for spending to a foundation, which then on their behalf can collect research projects or artistic works—protected by bureaucratic organization and corporate responsibility from imputations of extravagance. (As I write this, however, the big foundations such as Ford and Rockefeller are under Congressional Committee scrutiny—there seems to be no escape from money save anonymity!)

Another form of putting spending at arm's length is to delegate it to one's children. Whether for toys or for schools, for space in the home or advice on child management, more money is being spent on children and by them than ever before. The trouble with children, of course, is that they grow up—unlimited amounts cannot be spent on them. Before too long, in the same strata that Veblen and Arthur Miller have influenced, the children now grown up are denouncing advertising and disdainful of waste and extravagance. The parents, of course, can have more children, and as you may know, this is what has happened to the country in the last decade, much to the bewilderment of the demographers, who thought that the

American urban middle classes would continue to have fewer and fewer children and more and more commodities. Demographers do not know, and I do not know, why the shift has occurred; doubtless the causes are complex and ramified—the same thing has happened in France and elsewhere. But I do suspect that the changes in value-patterns we have been discussing have been among the factors. I started several years ago reading college class books for the light they might shed on subtle shifts in attitude. I was struck by the emphasis on the family that began to appear in my own and other college classes of a few years back. People in writing about themselves no longer started off by saying they were Vice-President of Ozark Air Lines and a director of the Tulsa National Bank, and so forth; they began by telling about the wife and five kids and how they had a home in the suburbs where they all enjoyed barbecues in the back yard. The occupational achievement was played down; the family scene, with its pastoral virtues, played up. Since then I have found similar tendencies in other groups. This would seem to hang together with the devaluation of individual success we have been discussing: children are a kind of unequivocal good in a world of changing values, and we can lavish on children the care and emotions we would now feel it egotistical to lavish on ourselves. The younger age at which people are marrying today is a further factor; having started to go steady at fourteen, they want to settle down at twenty. Whereas a generation ago a career man and a career girl would have considered marriage an obstacle to their work aims, today marriage and children are in a way part of the consumption and leisure sphere, the side of life currently emphasized.

Thus, children absorb some of the surplus and foundations some more of it. Especially the biggest foundation of all—the federal government. Conspicuous consumption has been socialized, and appears of necessity largely in the form of weapons, with something left over for national parks. When we speak of government spending for armaments, it is clear that the line between consumption and production is hard to draw, and the much more general point I want to make is that with the decline in conspicuous consumption—a relative rather than an absolute decline perhaps—has come a great rise in what we might call conspicuous production.

As I have implied earlier, the company for which Willy Loman worked did not engage in conspicuous production—else they would have kept him on, finding a place for him in overhead. The companies that do engage in it begin by locating and designing their plants and offices for show as well as for "efficiency" in the older sense of nearness to suppliers, distributors, and other facilities. It would be interesting to know to what extent the immense tax-facilitated rebuilding of American industry since World War II has been influenced by management's desire to have a plant that looked like the *Fortune* ads of the Austin Company and other designers of low-slung, "streamlined" factories. To be sure, if such factories are good for morale, they are by definition efficient, but the Hawthorne experiments are some evidence that workers respond more to interest taken in them than to lighting, cooling, or other circumambient factors—very likely, such factories are good for executives' and directors' morale. (These experiments were made nearly a generation ago and it may be that the subtle relations between the effects of physical and social environment have altered since then.)

Conspicuous production takes a great variety of forms. If a company leads the procession in granting paid vacations or in providing some new service for employees—that may be partly conspicuous production. Many additions to overhead both constitute such production and spend time advertising it—even some incumbents of the president's chair may have that as their principal role. Officials, who would no longer be as eager as their predecessors were to buy their way into an exclusive country club, suburb, or resort, are most eager to have their companies' ads appear in the pages of *Business Week, Fortune,* or on television, whether or not their market research can wholly justify each instance of space- or time-buying. I understand that some large companies have issued manuals to their officials on how to live up to their expense accounts, and we may properly regard such manuals as successors to all the educative literature by which previous ruling groups have been taught to spend—something which, strange as it may seem to some of you, needs always to be learned.

Professor Richard Hofstadter has suggested that these practices should be called conspicuous corporate consumption rather than conspicuous production. Certainly, it is as difficult to distinguish one from the other as to distinguish work from play among many of the managerial workforce. It would take a very close scrutiny of factory lay-out, for instance, to be sure what changes were the result of desires for corporate prestige rationalized as cost-cutting methods, and to know whether to allocate the costs of prestige itself to the production or the consumption side of the ledger. The aesthetics of the machines of production, factories and plants express a slightly different kind of conspicuous production. It is only when we adopt an "economizing" point of view that we can distinguish, in the activities centered around the economy, between the end of maximizing the product and the other ends, ceremonial, religious, prestige-laden, that are contextually being pursued. The conspicousness of these other ends is the result, as Professor Martin Meyerson has pointed out to me, of our taking for granted as the sole end of work that of maximizing product—from that distorted, if traditional, perspective other ends embedded in the context of social life appear out of order, even garish. Men who in the nineteenth century or today have seemed to be pursuing wealth or efficiency as a single uncomplicated goal certainly have been self-deceived as to their total gamut of motives. Nevertheless we can say, I think, that corporate consumption, in which each company goes into business as a junior welfare state, does currently rearrange our motives in a new configuration.

One factor, as I have already indicated, is the increasing professionalization of management, a development which has had consequences rather different from those Brandeis or Taylor hoped for. The eighteenth- and nineteenth-century industrialist came out of a rural background or ideology: he regarded his firm as a farm, and his work-force as hired hands, often transient and easily replaced, or as a small-town business, paternalistically run. He did not think of himself as having to be an expert on human relations—that could be left to the clergy, the main professionals in his purview. Feeling, moreover, some doubt as to where he stood socially, vis-à-vis the clergy and vis-à-vis Eastern aristocrats, he built a big feudal castle of a house for himself to show everybody that he had arrived, as if to declaim that he was personally worthy by visible evidences of his net worth: if he could not outshout the clergyman and the statesman, he could at least outshine them. And his wife, lacking the cultural tutelage of aristocratic wives and excluded by patriarchal convention from any contact with the workaday world, had nothing more to occupy her than to act as his deputy in conspicuous spending, his ambassadress to the dominions of culture he was too busy and too bored to bother with.

Such an industrialist, when he met his competitors, frankly regarded them as such, and whatever conviviality he might show, he kept his secrets of production to himself. He met with others, that is, in terms of money, not in terms of a specialized profession which freely exchanges its own secrets while keeping them from the lay public. Today, the communication of industrialists and businessmen with one another is frequently quite different. Meeting as professionals, the former individuality which distinguished the American businessman is rubbed off. He seeks status in his ability to run a smooth, attractive, and pleasant social and technological organization. Unions obviously have done something to encourage this, and so has government, in its tax and labor policy, but the desire of businessmen themselves to become professionals in human relations seems to be a major element.

And their wives, too, have changed. If they are college trained, it isn't enough for them to spend their husband's income. Often they have had jobs themselves; they may be professionals in their own right, or potential professionals. They want to become pals and companions of their business spouses—sleeping partners, so to speak—aware of what goes on at work, and vicarious consumers of corporate conspicuousness, flaunting not so much their own now-standardized fur coats but their husbands' firms—a more indirect display. Both husband and wife are urban, not small-town and rural, in their orientation; and they tend to view the factory workforce as a human collectivity in which there are roles to be played and maneuvers to be made. The earlier nineteenth-century horrors of rapid urbanization, in which human relations tended to become depersonalized and older social groupings disintegrated, now appear to be giving way to new institutional forms adapted to the conditions of contemporary city life. The presence of women on this scene, in fact or in feeling, helps alter the atmosphere, introducing a consumption mood into work relations, with its refreshing congeniality of association as contrasted with a male society of tycoons.

The divorce of corporate ownership from control and the consequent disenfranchisement of the stockholders (plus federal tax policies) have put responsibility for spending the corporate surplus on the executive in his capacity as an official, for corporate savings are only to a limited extent distributed to stockholders but are increasingly retained in depreciation funds or other concealment or reserve accounts. Business management schools play a part in deciding what it is that the corporation should now spend money for—whether it is for training directors, or market research, or philanthropic activity (which now supports much "pure" research)—all the multifarious forms of conspicuous corporate consumption.

In general, I think it can be said that many of the motives which were in earlier decades built into the character structure of individuals are now built into the institutional structure of corporate life. On the whole, I would rather see our surplus used to allow individuals a still greater amount of leisure, so that each of us would work, let us say, a four-hour day, then keep us at work eight hours so that our large organizations can generously spend the difference. And yet, in making such a judgment, I know I must continuously keep in mind the complex and stratified nature of the changes going on in our American life. If I had to choose between having Lever Brothers spend the American surplus on its beautiful Park Avenue offices and having the Happy Lomans and Glenn McCarthys spend it, I could easily come down on the side of Lever Brothers. Corporate consumption may be, as it has often been in architecture, a pleasure in its own right and sometimes a model for individual consumption.

Chapter 7   A DISSENT FROM THE LEFT: THE OPPRESSION OF THE MIDDLE CLASS

C. WRIGHT MILLS *(1916-1962), professor of sociology at Columbia University, was not impressed by the glass palaces on Park Avenue or by the arguments of the consensus intellectuals about the changed attitudes of business managers and the social effects of the new prosperity. Mills revealed something of the temper of a nineteenth-century populist as well as the ideas of Karl Marx and Max Weber in his sociological writings such as* The Power Elite *(1956). He also anticipated in his polemical* The Causes of World War III *(1958) and* Listen Yankee *(1960) most of the arguments of alienated youth and anti-war protesters of the late 1960's and early 1970's, and he viewed business firms as essentially unreconstructed and oppressive. He saw their employees, notably the white-collar middle classes, as a new* lumpenproletariat *victimized by tedious, impersonal routines of work and suffering from malaise and political defencelessness. The angry Mills found no joy even in the leisure of modern man. The following two separate passages are taken from his best known book,* White Collar: The American Middle Classes *(1951), in which he concludes with a denunciatory explanation of the alleged political indifference of the 1950's.*

. . . . The troubles that confront the white-collar people are the troubles of all men and women living in the twentieth century. If these troubles seem particularly bitter to the new middle strata, perhaps that is because for a brief time these people felt themselves immune to trouble.

Before the First World War there were fewer little men, and in their brief monopoly of high-school education they were in fact protected from many of the sharper edges of the workings of capitalistic progress. They were free to entertain deep illusions about their individual abilities and about the collective trustworthiness of the system. As their number has grown, however, they have become increasingly subject to wage-worker conditions. Especially since the Great Depression have white-collar people come up against all the old problems of capitalist society. They have been racked by slump and war and even by boom. They have learned about impersonal unemployment in depressions and about impersonal death by technological violence in war. And in good times, as prices rose faster than salaries, the money they thought they were making was silently taken away from them.

The material hardship of nineteenth-century industrial workers finds its parallel on the psychological level among twentieth-century white-collar employees. The new Little Man seems to have no firm roots, no sure loyalties to sustain his life and give it a center. He is not aware of having any history, his past being as brief as it is unheroic; he has lived through no golden age he can recall in time of trouble. Perhaps because he does not know where he going, he is in a frantic hurry; perhaps because he does not know what frightens him, he is paralyzed with fear. This is especially a feature of his political life, where the paralysis results in the most profound apathy of modern times.

The uneasiness, the malaise of our time, is due to this root fact: in our politics and economy, in family life and religion—in practically every sphere of our existence—the certainties of the eighteenth and nineteenth centuries have disintegrated or been destroyed and, at the same time, no new sanctions or justifications for the new routines we live, and must live, have taken hold. So there is no acceptance and there is no rejection, no sweeping hope and no sweeping rebellion. There is no plan of life. Among white-collar people, the malaise is deep-rooted; for the absence of any order of belief has left them morally defenseless as individuals and politically impotent as a group. Newly created in a harsh time of creation, white-collar man has no culture to lean upon except the contents of a mass society that has shaped him and seeks to manipulate him to its alien ends. For security's sake, he must strain to attach himself somewhere, but no communities or organizations seem to be thoroughly his. This isolated position makes him excellent material for synthetic molding at the hands of popular culture—print, film, radio, and television. As a metropolitan dweller, he is especially open to the focused onslaught of all the manufactured loyalties and distractions that are contrived and urgently pressed upon those who live in worlds they never made.

In the case of the white-collar man, the alienation of the wage-worker from the products of his work is carried one step nearer to its Kafka-like completion. The salaried employee does not make anything, although he may handle much that he greatly desires but cannot have. No product of craftsmanship can be his to contemplate with pleasure as it is being created and after it is made. Being alienated from any product of his labor, and going year after year through the same paper routine, he turns his leisure all the more frenziedly to the *ersatz* diversion that is sold him, and partakes of the synthetic excitement that neither eases nor releases. He is bored at work and restless at play, and this terrible alternation wears him out.

In his work he often clashes with customer and superior, and must almost always be the standardized loser: he must smile and be personable, standing behind the counter, or waiting in the outer office. In many strata of white-collar employment, such traits as courtesy, helpfulness, and kindness, once intimate, are now part of the impersonal means of livelihood. Self-alienation is thus an accompaniment of his alienated labor.

When white-collar people get jobs, they sell not only their time and energy but their personalities as well. They sell by the week or month their smiles and their kindly gestures, and they must practice the prompt repression of resentment and aggression. For these intimate traits are of commercial relevance and required for the more efficient and profitable distribution of goods and services. Here are the new little Machiavellians, practicing their personable crafts for hire and for the profit of others, according to rules laid down by those above them.

In the eighteenth and nineteenth centuries, rationality was identified with freedom. The ideas of Freud about the individual, and of Marx about society, were strengthened by the assumption of the coincidence of freedom and rationality. Now rationality seems to have taken on a new form, to have its seat not in individual men, but in social institutions which by their bureaucratic planning and mathematical foresight usurp both freedom and rationality from the little individual men caught in them. The calculating hierarchies of department store and industrial corporation, of rationalized office and governmental bureau, lay out the gray ways of work and stereotype the permitted initiatives. And in all this bureaucratic usurpation of freedom and of rationality, the white-collar people are the interchangeable parts of the big chains of authority that bind the society together.

White-collar people, always visible but rarely seen, are politically voiceless. Stray politicians wandering in the political arena without party may put 'white collar' people alongside businessmen, farmers, and wage-workers in their broadside appeals, but no platform of either major party has yet referred to them directly. Who fears the clerk? Neither *Alice Adams* nor *Kitty Foyle* could be a *Grapes of Wrath* for the 'share-croppers in the dust bowl of business.'

But while practical politicians, still living in the ideological air of the nineteenth century, have paid little attention to the new middle class, theoreticians of the left have vigorously claimed the salaried employee as a potential proletarian, and theoreticians of the right and center have hailed him as a sign of the continuing bulk and vigor of the middle class. Stray heretics from both camps have even thought, from time to time, that the higher-ups of the white-collar world might form a center of initiative for new political beginnings. In Germany, the 'black-coated worker' was one of the harps that Hitler played on his way to power. In England, the party of labor is thought to have won electoral socialism by capturing the votes of the suburban salaried workers.

To the question, what political direction will the white-collar people take, there are as many answers as there are theorists. Yet to the observer of American materials, the political problem posed by these people is not so much what the direction may be as whether they will take any political direction at all.

Between the little man's consciousness and the issues of our epoch there seems to be a veil of indifference. His will seems numbed, his spirit meager. Other men of other strata are also politically indifferent, but electoral victories are imputed to them; they do have tireless pressure groups and excited captains who work in and around the hubs of power, to whom, it may be imagined, they have delegated their enthusiasm for public affairs. But white-collar people are scattered along the rims of all the wheels of power: no one is enthusiastic about them and, like political eunuchs, they themselves are without potency and without enthusiasm for the urgent political clash.

Estranged from community and society in a context of distrust and manipulation; alienated from work and, on the personality market, from self; expropriated of individual rationality, and politically apathetic—these are the new little people, the unwilling vanguard of modern society. These are some of the circumstances for the acceptance of which their hopeful training has quite unprepared them. . . .

The distrust and the ambivalent status afforded the American politician has been rooted in the balloting system, which with its long list of unknown names allows the party machine to select loyal men of little or no worth to the community. Many of these party workers are pay-offs, who 'got things done' without publicity or formal sanction; others are selected precisely because they are 'weak sisters' and thus controllable as 'dummies' of the boss. The need of the boss and his machine for funds means that offices have often been sold and bought. Also, decentralized party control has made for 'a premium on parochialism' in national leaders: men, usually governors, who have carefully refrained from committing themselves on national and international issues are pumped up during the campaign to a national status they have by no means earned. The dominance and the near sacrosanct character of the business system have meant that when things go wrong in the political economy, blame is displaced from the businessman to the politician. The successful candidate, therefore, tends to be selected from among the uncommitted and the mediocre.

Brighter men have found more suitable careers outside politics and the people have become uninterested in politics. The exception to both has probably occurred only in situations in which the politician has been forced to act—as in slump or war. Lincoln, Wilson, and Franklin Roosevelt found themselves in such situations, and the general status impugnment of politicians has not touched them with its usual force.

In our day, muckraking, despite the glaring need for it, is properly seen as 'an integral part of an era, an era that ended with the soggy public response to the Teapot Dome disclosures.' No longer can a Lincoln Steffens command attention by detailed proof that "in a country where business is dominant, businessmen will corrupt a government which can pass laws to hinder or help business.' That, as Walter Shannon puts it, is now 'old stuff,' which is to say, that people cynically accept it rather than revolt against it.

Conflicts within the social structure have not been fully articulated in the political sphere; great changes have occurred without benefit of any political struggle. The U. S. political order has been continuous for more than a century and a half, and for this continuity it has paid the price of many internal compromises and adjustments without explicit reformulations of principle or symbol. Its institutions have been greatly adaptive; its traditions, expedient; its great figures, inveterate opportunists.

The American political order has never known deeply situated movements, or parties with the will and the chance to change the whole political structure. For a hundred and sixty years parties have argued over symbols and issues concerned with who got what within the prevailing system. There has been no relatively successful 'third party' which questioned that system, and so no indigenous political theory which might proceed with such a movement. American politics has bred the opportunistic politician in the compromised party in the two-party state.

Each of the two parties must appeal to diverse interests and variegated strata and therefore may articulate only generalized, widely accepted issues. Neither can afford to articulate explicit views or the interests of specific groups; and their competition leads to universal appeals and hence to many broken pledges, to a universal rhetoric of vacuity rather than conflicting ideologies of particular strata. The more variegated the public to which the patronage party must appeal for support, the more empty of decisive, antagonistic content its programs will be. It blunts the issues it reflects, attenuates the desires it serves. In its fear of alarming anyone, it talks while managing to say nothing. So lively issues, closely connected with everyday reality, are not presented in the controversies of the parties. Trotsky, in quite another context, once wrote: "A party for whom everybody votes except that minority who know what they re voting for, is no more a party, than the tongue in which babies in all countries babble is a national language.'

Political selection, for the electorate, comment the Lynds, 'becomes a matter of lining up on one side or the other of an either-or situation. The issues involved in supporting the eithers or the ors have become somewhat more blurred since the 'nineties . . .' And because of this artificial party situation, 'elections are no longer the lively centers of public interest they were in the 'nineties. In 1890 Middletown gave itself over for weeks before each election to the bitter, hilarious joy of conflict . . . Today torchlight processions and horns no longer blast out the voters or usher in the newly elected officials, and, although speeches persist with something of their old vigor, new inventions offering a variety of alternate interests are pressing upon politics as upon lodges, unions, and churches.'

The compromises in the two-party state tend to occur within the party formations; when they do occur between the parties, they often take the form of non-publicized, even non-publicizable, deals. So popular will is less effective than the pressure of organized minorities; where power is already distributed in extremely disproportionate ways, the principle of hidden compromise is likely to work for the already powerful.

The *compromising* party means, ideally at least, that two groups, each representing definite, antagonistic interests, integrate policy as best they can in order to realize all the existent interests possible. How well they can succeed in this depends in large part upon how deep the antagonisms are. The *compromised* party, on the other hand, refers to a party in which there has been so much expediency and compromise going on *within* it that its leaders really can't do anything decisive or stand up and say No to anybody. Party managers minimize the public discussion of fundamental issues; politicians solve them by means of the personal contact and the private integration. The compromised party is everybody's friend.

There is usually very little real difference between the two major U. S. parties, yet together they virtually monopolize the chances at political organization and political propaganda on a large scale. This party system is ideal for a people that is largely contented, which is to say that such a people need not be interested in politics as a struggle for the power to solve real issues.

Such political contentment as has prevailed is no doubt aided by the general fact of occupational, pecuniary, and social ascent, but more specifically, the potential leaders of the lower ranks have had, in each generation, available channels of upward mobility. In this way, as Gunnar Myrdal has shown, they have been drained off as opposition leaders. In the two-party system probably 'the best men' go into the dominant and long-established local party. The latest channel, open in this way, has been the big labor unions that came out of the great depression. These unions have quickly been bureaucratized, in many ways tamed; but they have provided new ways up, to higher income, prestige, and power, for many 'militant' young men, working-class boys who could adapt their views to the organizational practices of the unions. In so far as organizers and articulate spokesmen of definite interests might increase general political alertness, this draining of talent from the lower circles has decreased their chances to become alert.

Most political decisions of consequence have been moved from local to state to federal establishment. The issues of local politics, to which the individual might be supposed most alert, have become in some part a matter of deals between federal powers and local authorites. 'During the 'twenties,' says a liberal organization's leader, 'you could get together local pressures to squeeze Congress. During the 'thirties, you didn't need it so much. It was there at the center, and we got dependent on it. Then the war stymied political efforts . . . Now, just a while ago, we wanted wide support for a bill, but we couldn't find any. There just aren't any local organizations or local fire any more. They've withered away.'

The distance between the individual and centers of power has become greater, and the individual has come to feel powerless. Between political hope and political realization there are the two parties and the federal bureaucracy, which, as means of political action, often seem to cut the nerve of direct political interest. Indifference may thus be seen as an understandable response to a condition of powerlessness. In Barbara Wootton's words, ' "Political apathy" may be the expression of a sort of horse-sense. It may be the indifference not so much of those who can, but will not, as of those who realize when they cannot—a refusal, in fact, to attempt a response to demands that are recognized to be impossible.' There is a felt lack of power between the individual's everyday life and what is going on in the distant worlds of politics. . . .

By virtue of their increased and centralized power, political institutions become more objectively important to the course of American history, but because of mass alienation, less and less of subjective interest to the population at large. On the one hand, politics is bureaucratized, and on the other, there is mass indifference. These are the decisive aspects of U.S. politics today. Because of them, political expression is banalized, political theory is barren administrative detail, history is made behind men's backs. Such is the political situation in which the new middle classes enact their passive role. . . .

Chapter 8 PLURALISM AND MORAL ISSUES

DANIEL BELL *(1919-   ), former labor editor of*
Fortune *and now professor of sociology at Harvard Uni-*
versity, vigorously criticized C. Wright Mills' thesis of a
tuling "power elite," contending instead in The End of
Ideology *(1960) that American politics was based upon an*
extraordinary pluralism and the skills of compromise. Bell
and other leading intellectuals who are identified with the
consensus school of the 1950's, including Richard Hofstadter,
Daniel Boorstin, Louis Hartz, and Seymour Lipset, differed
on certain issues but concurred that the absence of a feudal
past, class struggles, and religious strife distinguished the
American from the European experience. Bell, the author of
a scholarly history of American socialism, called particular
attention to the failure of left-wing movements to establish
themselves in the United States. Addressing the phenomenon
of McCarthyism, he contended that it involved a novel
introduction of moral issues into public affairs but anticipated
than an open society could absorb this "new threat." In a
concluding chapter from The End of Ideology, *not reprinted*
below, Bell observed that the old radicalism had lost its meaning,
but noted the emergence of a "new Left" which looked to
Cuba, Africa, and "revolution" in its angry and almost
desperate search for a cause. Bell urged instead, as typified
in the selection presented here, an end to rhetoric of revolu-
tionary violence and a recognition of "old verities" and
human values. Thus was forecast the clash of a decade later.

. . . . From the viewpoint of the mass-society hypothesis, the United States ought to be exceptionally vulnerable to the politics of disaffection. In our country, urbanization, industrialization, and democratization have eroded older primary and community ties on a scale unprecedented in social history. Yet, though large-scale unemployment during the depression was more prolonged and more severe here than in any country in Western Europe, the Communist movement never gained a real foothold in the United States, nor has any fascist movement on a European model arisen. How does one explain this?

It is asserted that the United States is an "atomized" society composed of lonely, isolated individuals. One forgets the truism, expressed sometimes as a jeer, that Americans are a nation of joiners. There are in the United States today at least 200,000 voluntary organizations, associations, clubs, societies, lodges, and fraternities, with an aggregate (but obviously overlapping) membership of close to 80 million men and women. In no other country in the world, probably, is there such a high degree of voluntary communal activity, expressed sometimes in absurd rituals, yet often providing real satisfactions for real needs.

"It is natural for the ordinary American," wrote Gunnar Myrdal, "when he sees something that is wrong to feel not only that there should be a law against it, but also that an organization should be formed to combat it." Some of these voluntary organizations are pressure groups—business, farm, labor, veterans, trade associations, the aged, etc.—but thousands more are like the National Association for the Advancement of Colored People, the American Civil Liberties Union, the League of Women Voters, the American Jewish Committee, the Parent-Teachers Associations, local community-improvement groups, and so on, each of which affords hundreds of individuals concrete, emotionally shared activities.

Equally astonishing are the number of ethnic group organizations in this country carrying on varied cultural, social, and political activites. The number of Irish, Italian, Jewish, Polish, Czech, Finnish, Bulgarian, Bessarabian, and other national groups, their hundreds of fraternal, communal, and political groups, each playing a role in the life of America, is staggering.

Even in urban neighborhoods, where anonymity is presumed to flourish, the extent of local ties is astounding. Within the city limits of Chicago, for example, there are 82 community newspapers with a total weekly circulation of almost one million; within Chicago's larger metropolitan area, there are 181. According to standard sociological theory, these local papers providing news and gossip about neighbors should slowly decline under the pressure of the national media. Yet the reverse is true. In Chicago, the number of such newspapers has increased 165 per cent since 1910; in those forty years, circulation has jumped 770 per cent. As sociologist Morris Janowitz, who studied these community newspapers, observed: "If society were as impersonal, as self-centered and barren as described by some who are preoccupied with the one-way trend from 'Gemeinschaft' to 'Gesellschaft' seem to believe, the levels of criminality, social disorganization and psychopathology which social science seeks to account for would have to be viewed as very low rather than (as viewed now) alarmingly high."

It may be argued that the existence of such a large network of voluntary associations says little about the cultural level of the country concerned. It may well be, as Ortega maintains, that cultural standards throughout the world have declined (in everything?—in architecture, dress, design?), but nonetheless a greater proportion of the population today participates in worthwhile cultural activities. This has been almost an inevitable concomitant of the doubling—literally—of the American standard of living over the last fifty years.

The rising levels of education have meant a rising appreciation of culture. In the

United States, more dollars are spent on concerts of classical music than baseball. Sales of books have doubled in a decade. There are over a thousand symphony orchestras, and several hundred museums, institutes and colleges are purchasing art in the United States today. Various other indexes can be cited to show the growth of a vast middlebrow society. And in coming years, with steadily increasing productivity and leisure, the United States will become an even more active "consumer" of culture.

It has been argued that the American mass society imposes an excessive conformity upon its members. But it is hard to discern who is conforming to what. The *New Republic* cries that "hucksters are sugarcoating the culture." The *National Review*, organ of the "radical right," raises the banner of iconoclasm against the domination of opinion-making in our society by "the liberals." *Fortune* decries the growth of "organization man." Each of these tendencies exists, yet in historical perspective there is probably less conformity to an over-all mode of conduct today than at any time within the last half century in America. True, there is less bohemianism than in the twenties (though increased sexual tolerance) and less political radicalism than in the thirties (though the New Deal enacted sweeping reforms). But does the arrival at a political dead center mean the establishment, too, of a dead norm? I do not think so. One would be hard put to find today the "conformity" *Main Street* exacted of Carol Kennicott thirty years ago. With rising educational levels, more individuals are able to indulge a wider variety of interests. ("Twenty years ago you couldn't sell Beethoven out of New York," reports a record salesman. "Today we sell Palestrina, Monteverdi, Gabrielli, and Renaissance and Baroque music in large quantities.")

The curious fact, perhaps, is that no one in the United States defends conformity. Everyone is against it, and probably everyone always was. Thirty-five years ago, you could easily rattle any middle-class American by charging him with being a "Babbitt." Today you can do so by accusing him of conformity. The problem is to know who is accusing whom. In December, 1958, the *Reader's Digest* (circulation twelve million) reprinted an article from *Woman's Day* (circulation five million) with the title, "The Danger of Being Too Well-Adjusted." The point of the article is that great men were not adjusted, and the article quotes a psychiatrist who says that "we've made conformity into a religion"; we ought to remember, however, that each child is different "and ought to be."

Such citation is no proof that there is not "conformity" in the middle class; but if there is, there is also a great deal of anxiety and finger-pointing about it. Certainly those who live on the margin of society—the Upper Bohemians, whose manners soon become the style for the culture—seek frantically to find different ways of emphasizing their non-conformity. In Hollywood, where Pickfair society in the twenties counterfeited a European monarchy (and whose homes crossed Louis XIV with Barnum & Bailey), "non-conformity," according to *Life* magazine (in its jumbo Entertainment issue of December 22, 1958—readership twenty-five million), "is now the key to social importance and that Angry Middle-Aged man, Frank Sinatra, is its prophet and reigning social monarch." The Sinatra set, *Life* points out, deliberately mocks the old Hollywood taboos and is imitated by a host of other sets that eagerly want to be non-conformist as well. Significantly—a fact *Life* failed to mention—the reigning social set and its leaders, Sinatra, Dean Martin, Sammy Davis, Jr., are all from minority groups and from the wrong side of the tracks. Sinatra and Martin are Italian, Davis a Negro. In earlier times in American life, a minority group, having bulled its way to the top, would usually ape the style and manners of the established status community. In Hollywood, the old status hierarchies have been fragmented, the new sets celebrate their triumph by jeering at the pompous ways of the old.

At the margins of the literary life, and a different social phenomenon, are the Beatniks, a hopped-up, jazzed-up, souped-up, self-proclaimed group of outcasts who are rebelling against the "highly organized academic and literary movement employment agency of the Neoanti-reconstructionist [who form] a dense crust of custom over American cultural life." But the singular fact is, as Delmore Schwartz recently argued, that these beatniks are imaginary rebels, "since the substance of their work is a violent advocacy of a nonconformism which they already possess . . . since non-conformism of almost every variety had become acceptable and respectable and available to everyone. Unlike the Bohemianism of the past, which had to attack the dominant Puritanism and Victorianism of respectable society in a variety of forms, including the censorship of books, Prohibition and a prudery enforced by the police, the new nonconformism has no genuine enemy . . . hence the new rebel bears a great deal of resemblance to a prize fighter trying to knock out an antagonist who is not in the ring with him." The additional sardonic fact is that the man in the gray flannel suit, the presumed target of the Beatniks, is, as Russel Lynes pointed out, especially if he is in advertising, or the entertainment media, an Upper Bohemian himself. The job is accepted as a means of obtaining an income in order to sport and flaunt his presumed, idiosyncratic tastes in dress, food, travel, and the like. The problem for all these multiple sets is not conformity but added novelty.

To add one more paradox, the early theorists of mass society (e.g., Simmel) condemned it because in the vast metropolitan honeycombs people were isolated, transient, anonymous to each other. Americans, sensitive as they are to the criticism of others, took the charge to heart and, in building the postwar suburbs, sought to create fraternity, communality, togetherness, only to find themselves accused of conformity. In the new, recent trend of people returning to the city, it is clear that, in recoil, people will once again establish barriers and will thus bring on the charge, in the next inspection by European sociology, of anonymity, isolation and soullessness, and *anomie*. . . .

The multiplication of interests and the fractioning of groups, occurring simultaneously with the breakup of the older family capitalism and the rise of new managerial groups to power within the business enterprises, make it difficult to locate the sources of political power in the United States. More than ever, government in the U.S. has become, in John Chamberlain's early phrase, "the broker state." To say that this is a broker state does not mean, however, that all interests have equal power. This is a business society. But within the general acceptance of corporate capitalism, modified by union power and checked by government control, the deals and interest-group trading proceeds.

Granting the viability of these conventional lines of political analysis—the role of the two-party system in limiting social movements and social clashes, the political tradition of direct appeal to the people, and the force of interest-groups in shaping and modifying legislative policy—they nevertheless leave us somewhat ill-equippped to understand the issues which have dominated the politics of the 1950's decade. These lines of thought do not help us, for example, to understand the Communist issue, the forces behind the new nationalism of, say, Senators Bricker and Know-land, and the momentary range of support and the intense emotional heat generated by Senator McCarthy. In short, what has traditionally been called "interest-group" politics does not help to explain the emergence of the new American right wing, the group that S. M. Lipset has dubbed the "radical right"—radical because it opposes traditional conservatism, with its respect for individual rights, and because it sought to impose new patterns in American life. All this is dramatized by the issue of McCarthy and the Communists.

For Europeans, particularly, the Communist issue must be a puzzle. After all, there is no mass Communist party in the United States such as one finds in France and Italy; the Communist party in the U.S. never, at any single moment, had more than 100,000 members. In the last five years, when the Communist issue entered the national scene, the Communists had already lost most of the political influence they once had. The Communist unions had been expelled from the CIO*; the Progressive party, repudiated by Henry Wallace, had fizzled; and they were fast losing strength in the intellectual community.

It is true that liberals have tended to play down the Communist issue. And the contradictory stand of the Truman administration compounded these confusions and increased the alarms: on the one hand, leading members of the administration, including Truman himself, sought to minimize the degree of past Communist infiltration; on the other hand, the administration let loose a buckshot charge of security regulations which had little regard for personal liberties and rights. The invasion of South Korea and the emotional reaction against the Chinese and Russian Communists, which carried over to domestic Communists; the disclosures, particularly by Whittaker Chambers, of the infiltration of Communists into high posts in gov-

*By 1952, at the height of McCarthyism, the Communists controlled unions with fewer than five per cent of U.S. labor membership as against a peak control of unions with twenty per cent of union membership in 1944.

ernment and the existence of espionage rings; and, finally, the revelations in the Canadian spy investigations, in the Allan Nunn May trial in Britain, and in the Rosenberg case that the Soviets had stolen U.S. atom secrets, all played a role in heightening national tension.

But even after the natural effects of all these are taken into account, it is difficult to explain the unchallenged position so long held by Senator McCarthy. It still fails to take into account the extensive damage to the democratic fabric that McCarthy and others were able to cause on the Communist issue, as well as the reckless methods disproportionate to the problem: the loyalty oaths on campuses, the compulsive Americanism which saw threats to the country in the wording of a Girl Scout handbook, the violent clubbing of the Voice of America (which under the sensible leadership of anti-Communists, such as Bertram D. Wolfe, had conducted intelligent propaganda in Europe), the wild headlines and the senseless damaging of the Signal Corps radar research program at Fort Monmouth—in short, the suspicion and miasma of fear that played so large a role in American politics. Nor can conventional political analysis shed much light on him or his supporters. Calling him a demagogue explains little; the relevant questions arise in relation to whom and what he was demagogic about. McCarthy's targets were indeed strange. Huey Long, the last major demagogue, had vaguely attacked the rich and sought to "share the wealth." McCarthy's targets were intellectuals, expecially Harvard men, Anglophiles, internationalists, the Army.

But these targets provide the important clues to the right-wing support, a "radical right," that backed him, and the reasons for that support. These groups constituted a strange mélange: a thin stratum of soured patricians like Archibald Roosevelt, the last surviving son of Theodore Roosevelt, whose emotional stake lay in a vanishing image of a muscular American defying a decadent Europe; the "new rich"—the automobile dealers, real estate manipulators, oil wildcatters—who needed the psychological assurance that they, like their forebears, had earned their own wealth, rather than (as in fact) through government aid, and who feared that "taxes" would rob them of that wealth; the rising middle-class strata of the various ethnic groups, especially the Irish and the Germans, who sought to prove their Americanism (the Germans particularly because of the implied taint of disloyalty during World War II); and, finally, unique in U.S. cultural history, a small group of intellectuals, some of them cankered ex-Communists, who pivoting on McCarthy, opened up an attack on liberalism in general.

If this strange coalition, bearing the "sword of the Lord and Gideon," cannot be explained in the conventional terms that are applied to American politics, what can? One key concept is the idea of "status politics," an idea which has been used by Richard Hofstadter to deal with the status anxieties of the old aristocracy, and by S. M. Lipset with the status fears of the new rich.

The central idea of the status politics conception is that groups that are advancing in wealth and social position are often as anxious and politically feverish as groups that have become *déclasseé*. Many observers have noted that those groups which have lost their social position seek more violently than ever to impose on all groups the older values of a society which they once represented. Lipset has demonstrated that groups on the rise, in order to establish themselves, may insist on a similar conformity. This rise takes place in periods of prosperity, when class or economic interest-group conflicts have lost much of their force. And Hofstadter has argued further that economic issues take on importance in American political history only during the depressions, while in periods of prosperity "status" issues emerge. But these issues, usually "patriotic" in character, are amorphous and ideological.

These political forces, by their very nature, are unstable. McCarthy himself, by the logic of his own political position, and by the nature of his personality, had to go to an extreme. And he ended, finally, by challenging Eisenhower. It was McCarthy's great gamble. And he lost, for the challenge to a Republican president by a Republican minority could only have split the party. Faced with this threat, the party rallied behind Eisenhower, and McCarthy himself was isolated. In this respect, the events prove the soundness of the thesis of Walter Lippmann and the Alsops in 1952 that only a Republican president could provide the necessary continuity of foreign and domestic policy initiated and maintained by the Fair Deal. A Democratic president might have polarized the parties and given the extreme Republican wing the license to lead the attack; the administration of a moderate Republican could act as a damper on the extreme right.

The lessening of international tensions after the settlement in Korea confirmed McCarthy's defeat. Yet McCarthy has to be understood in relation to the people behind him and the changed political temper which these groups have brought. He was the catalyst, not the explosive force. These forces still remain. . . .

Few "symbols" are more representative of this change than the role of Dean Acheson. In the early days of the New Deal, Acheson, a young lawyer, resigned as Assistant Secretary of the Treasury in protest against the "tinkering" with the dollar and the departure from orthodox practices; and Acheson was one of the symbols of conservative protest against the New Deal. A decade and a half later, as Truman's Secretary of State, he had become the symbol of the "radical" policies of the Fair Deal. In those terms, of course, the conceptualization was meaningless.

But the fact that the arena of politics was now foreign policy allowed the moralistic strains to come to the fore. One of the unique aspects of American politics is that while domestic issues have been argued in hard-headed, practical terms, with a give-and-take compromise as the outcome, foreign policy has always been phrased in moralistic terms. Perhaps the very nature of our emergence as an independent country forced us to constantly adopt a moral posture in regard to the rest of the world; perhaps being distant from the real centers of interest conflict allowed us to employ pieties, rather than face realities. But since foreign policy has usually been within the frame of moral rather than pragmatic discourse, the debate in the fifties became centered in moral terms. And the singular fact about the Communist problem is that, on a scale rare in American political life, an ideological issue was equated with a moral issue and the attacks on communism were made with all the compulsive moral fervor which was possible because of the equation of communism with sin.

In itself this reflects a curious change in American life. While we gain a more relaxed attitude towards private morals, we are becoming rather more extremist in public life.

The "ideologizing" of politics gains reinforcement from another, independent tendency in American life, the emergence of what may be called the "symbolic groups." These are the inchoate entities known generally in capital letters as "Labor," "Business," the "Farmers," et al. The assumption is made that these entities have a coherent philosophy, a defined purpose, and that they represent tangible forces. This tendency derives from varied sources, but the biggest impetus has come from the changing nature of economic decision-making and the changing mode of opinion-formation in modern society. The fact that major economic decision-making has been centralized in the narrow cockpit of Washington, rather than spread over the impersonal market, leads groups like the National Association of Manufacturers, the Farm Bureau, the American Federation of Labor, etc., to speak for "Business," for "Labor," for the "Farmers." At the same time there is an increased sensitivity to "Public Opinion," heightened by the use of opinion polls in which the "Citizen" (not the specific individual with his specific interests) is asked what "Business" or "Labor" or the "Farmer" should do. In effect, these groups are obeyond what they normally do.

Political debate, therefore, moves from specific clashes of interest, in which issues can be identified and possibly compromised, to ideologically tinged conflicts which polarize the various groups and divide the society.

The tendency to convert concrete issues into ideological problems, to invest them with moral color and high emotional charge, is to invite conflicts which can only damage a society. "A nation, divided irreconcilably on 'principle,' each party believing itself pure white and the other pitch black, cannot govern itself," wrote Walter Lippmann many years ago.

It has been one of the glories of the United States that politics has always been a pragmatic give-and-take rather than a series of wars-to-the-death. One ultimately comes to admire the "practical politics" of Theodore Roosevelt and his scorn for the intransigents, like Godkin and Villard, who, refusing to yield to expediency, could never put through their reforms. Politics, as Edmund Wilson has described T. R.'s attitude, "is a matter of adapting oneself to all sorts of people and situations, a game in which one may score but only by accepting the rules and recognizing one's opponents, rather than a moral crusade in which one's stainless standard must mow the enemy down."

Democratic politics means bargaining between legitimate groups and the search for consensus. . . .

But representative government is important for the deeper reason that by including all representative interests one can keep alive "the antagonism of influences which is the only real security for continued progress." It is the only way of securing the "concurrent majorities," which, as Calhoun argued, was the solid basis for providing a check on the tyrannical "popular" majority. For only through representative government can one achieve consensus—and conciliation.

This is not to say that the Communist "interest" is a legitimate one, akin to the interest of other groups in the society, or that the Communist issue was completely irrelevant. As a conspiracy, rather than a legitimate dissenting group, the Communist movement remains a threat to democratic society. And by the criteria of "clear and present danger" democratic society may at times have to act against that conspiracy. But these are questions to be handled by law. The tendency to use the Communist issue as a political club against other parties or groups, or the tendency to convert questions of law into issues of morality (and thus shift the source of sanctions from the courts and legitimate authority to private individuals) can only create strains in a liberal society.

In the 170 years since its founding, American democracy has been rent only once by civil war. We have learnt since then, not without strain, to include the "excluded interests," the workers and the small farmers. These have secured a legitimate place in the American political equilibrium. And the ideological conflicts that almost threatened to disrupt the society, in the early years of the New Deal, have been mitigated.

The new divisions, created by the status anxieties of new middle-class groups, pose a new threat. The rancors of McCarthyism were one of its ugly excesses. However, the United States, so huge and complex that no single political boss or any single political group has ever been able to dominate it, will in time undoubtedly diminish these divisions, too. This is an open society, and these anxieties are part of the price we pay for that openness.

Chapter 9 CONSERVATISM AND THE RESTRAINT OF POWER

*During the 1950's a battery of journalists and academic
intellectuals, some of whom were avowed
conservatives, vigorously assailed the long-dominant
liberals and their assumptions. Young conservative
editors, such as William F. Buckley, Jr., engaged in
sharp debates with liberal ideologues; and economists
such as Professor Milton Friedman questioned the
social-welfare philosophy and systems of economic
controls that had emerged during the presidency of
Harry S. Truman; and a cadre of political
philosophers and sociological theorists, several of
European background, questioned the fundamental
bases of liberal thought. One of the best known of
the conservative intellectuals in the 1950's was
Professor RUSSELL KIRK (1918-   ), a student of
Edmund Burke, historian of American conservatism,
philosopher, and publicist. His major writings include*
Randolph of Roanoke, *(1951),* The Conservative
Mind, *(1953), and* A Program for Conservatives,
(1954). In the following selection, taken from The
Intelligent Woman's Guide to Conservatism *(1957),
Kirk explains the need for checks on arbitrary
power—a theme that radicals espoused ten years later
but for different reasons.*

. . . . Scarcely any political aphorism is more widely quoted today than Lord
Acton's observation that "power tends to corrupt, and absolute power corrupts
absolutely"; yet the barriers against concentration of power—political power and
economic power—are steadily reduced in our age, throughout almost all the world,
with little effectual protest. The conservative, intent upon preserving order and
justice and freedom, does what he can to remind the modern world of the truth of
Acton's statement, and to retain those checks upon arbitrary power which distinguish a free society from a servile society.

The American War of Independence was the result of the colonists' protest that
Parliament was usurping to itself powers anciently reserved to the several colonies.
The Federalist Papers, which are the chief American contribution to the literature

Russell Kirk, *The Intelligent Woman's Guide to Conservatism* (New York: Devin-Adair, 1957),
pp. 75-83. Reprinted by permission.

of politics, are permeated with the conviction that power must be hedged, limited, reserved, kept in balance. The Federal Constitution, in essence, is an instrument for checking and balancing political power: the powers of federal and state governments, the powers of political authority and of private citizens, the powers of executive and legislative and judiciary. The practical understanding of the problem of power that was manifested by American statesmen like John Adams and James Madison has left its mark upon our institutions to this day.

Power, politically speaking, is the ability to do as one likes, regardless of the wills of one's fellows and neighbors. A state in which an individual or a small group are able to dominate the wills of their fellows without check is a despotism, whether it is called "monarchical" or "aristocratic" or "democratic." When every person claims to be a power unto himself, then a society is in anarchy. Anarchy never lasts long, being intolerable to everyone, and contrary to the inescapable fact that some persons are more strong and more clever than their neighbors. To anarchy there always succeeds tyranny or oligarchy, in which power is monopolized by a very few. The conservative endeavors so to limit and balance political power that anarchy or tyranny cannot arise. But men and women, in every age, are tempted to disregard the limitations upon power for the sake of some fancied temporary advantage. It is characteristic of the radical that he thinks of power as a force for good—so long as the power falls into his hands. In the name of liberty, the French and Russian revolutionaries abolished the old restrictions upon power; but power cannot be abolished; it always finds its way into someone's control; and, in France at the end of the eighteenth century and in Russia at the beginning of the twentieth century, the power which the revolutionaries had thought oppressive in the hands of the old regime became many times as tyrannical in the hands of the radical new masters of the state, who had stripped away what checks upon power the French and Russian monarchies never had dared to tamper with.

In some degree, nearly all men and women desire power; and with some persons, the desire for power is an overweening lust. No passion is more powerful than this. It is one of the errors of Marxism to exaggerate the importance of the economic motive in society. Most men and women, indeed, do desire material possessions. But many persons are much fonder of power than they are of wealth. One of the chief reasons for the acquring of wealth, for that matter, is that wealth often means power. The conservative, looking upon human nature as a mixture of good and evil, capable sometimes of high nobility, yet always in some sense flawed, knows that the thirst for power among us never will be quenched. No matter how prosperous or how nearly equal men and women are, they always will seek power. Accepting that sorry fact, the conservative seeks to set bounds to this power-appetite by ethical instruction and by good laws.

If only private property were abolished, some radical reformers have insisted, then mankind would be happy: because property, they have contended, is the root of all evil. If only social privilege were abolished, other radical reformers have declared, then mankind would be emancipated from envy and unjust ambition; because privilege, they have thought, is the source of man's inhumanity to man. These notions tended to dominate the liberal era of the past century and a half, and they are influential among us still. But they are fallacies. Property is sought by the unscrupulous not so much for its own sake as for the sake of the power which property generally confers. Privilege is sought by the unscrupulous much more for the sake of the power which it veils than for the sake of mere ostentation. If property and privilege and all the old motives to integrity and incentives to diligence which have been the characteristics of Western civlization were abolished tomorrow, still the fierce disagreement between man and man would continue; indeed, it probably would rage still more fiercely; for when only power remains as a gratification to ambition, then power will be the more ardently desired and the more ruthlessly pursued. And no one, I repeat, ever succeeds in abolishing power. Like energy, power is not dissipated; it merely changes forms.

In that terrible novel *1984*, George Orwell describes a society, merely a generation distant from our era, in which the only remaining gratification for the stronger and more talented natures is the possession of power. Religion is gone; privilege, in the old sense, is gone; private property is gone; liberal learning is gone; family life is gone; art is gone; philosophy is gone; simple contentment is gone. But there remains one ferocious motive to success, the lust after power. One sensation, in this society, still is pleasurable; the sensation of stamping forever on a human face. And the masters of this society so thoroughly enjoy this sensation that they consider it more than sufficient compensation for all that has been lost.

This is the triumph of a diabolical impulse, the ascendancy of Pride, the indulgence of that will to dominate one's fellows which Christian teaching always has endeavored to subdue. But Orwell's picture is not fantastic. We have seen within the past forty years the realization of this horrid regime in a great part of the world. A Socialist member of Parliament, returned from a visit to Poland, recently declared that he had seen in Soviet Poland the literal fulfillment of Orwell's fantasy. All the old checks on power had been abolished, together with all the old motives to integrity; and the consequence was a society by the side of which the most despotic government of the eighteenth century was gently liberal. All the humanitarian slogans of the Communists were of no weight when tossed into the balance against naked power.

Among a people who, like the Americans, have long been accustomed to an habitual and almost unconscious restraining and balancing of power—so long accustomed that they have nearly forgotten that such checks and balances exist—there is a perilous tendency to neglect the grim problem of power. Good will, economic reforms, and liberal slogans can remedy all the ills to which flesh is heir, the doctrinaire liberal argues; and many Americans, protected by national usage and sound constitutions from the more extreme risks of the pursuit of power, accept these arguments with little question. Thus, for instance, our foreign policy tends to degenerate into mere economic generosity—appropriation after appropriation for material assistance to "underdeveloped countries," or well-meant advice, accompanied by technical aid, to the leaders of Asia and Africa that if only they will struggle upward toward the American standard of living, internal disorder and international hostility will give way to the good society.

Now there are instances in which material assistance to other nations can achieve considerable benefits. But to assume that mere economic reform, of itself, can give peace to the nations is to ignore the whole ancient problem of power. And that problem, soon or late, refuses to be ignored. For economic gain is not the principal desire of most statesmen or of most nations. Prestige, glory, and especially power are more powerful motives. Among the nations which are reasonably prosperous, a sacrifice of some prosperity for a great deal of power often seems well worth while: thus Hitler successfully exhorted the Germans to exchange butter for guns. Among the nations which are deeply sunk in poverty, the possibility of any real and lasting improvement of their material condition is so remote that often they eagerly abandon this tiring struggle for the exciting pursuit of power.

In this, the Soviets have shown themselves more clever than we. For though the Communists profess "dialectical materialism" and material aggrandizement for the masses, in reality the masters of Soviet Russia play always the great grim game of power; their desire is domination, not universal prosperity; and they know how to play upon this ancient appetite for mastery over men and women. We promise ten times as much in economic assistance to the "underdeveloped countries" as the Russians do; we deliver a hundred times as much such assistance; and yet we have not been notably successful in our contest against Communist intrigue in Asia and Africa. For the Russians have played the game of power, while we have innocently practiced the materialism that the Russians preach. And, the desire for power being stronger than the desire for wealth among energetic men and women, the Soviets have touched chords in human nature which we Americans have neglected.

Now the conservative of reflection does not recommend that we ought to model our conduct upon successful Soviet intrigues. He does not believe that the unscrupulous encouragement of the appetite for power is a legitimate tactic of national interest. But he does realize that we cannot afford to leave out of our calculations, in foreign policy or in domestic, the ancient inclinations of the human heart. Men and women desire prestige, glory, power: very well, accept that fact, and try to direct that longing into ways of justice and order and freedom. Power, properly guarded and limited and channelled, is the means by which all improvement is undertaken. In itself, power is neither moral nor immoral: everything depends on the motives with which power is employed and the institutions which check its abuse. To treat other nations as if their only desires were material is to insult them grossly; even while accepting our assistance, under such circumstances, they will resent our presumption; and they will employ our assistance to play their own game of power. Justly checked and balanced power is respected and admired; unchecked and unscrupulous exercise of power is dreaded and envied; but neglected power is despised. These considerations, the conservative believes, ought to influence our foreign policy.

And our domestic policy ought also to be governed by a true apprehension of the nature of power. Men and women are not naturally good. Good and evil, rather, are intricately interwoven in their natures; and when the good predominates, it ordinarily is by virtue of emulation, habit, and obedience to just laws. If the old decencies, customs, and laws are swept away—no matter how generously humanitarian the excuse—the precarious balance of good over evil may be upset, and the old lust after power is released to work its old corruption. Constitutional restrictions, states' rights, local self-government, limitation upon executive authority, strict interpretation of the laws: all these devices to hedge and balance power often seem annoyingly old-fangled, particularly in an age of rapid economic expansion. The impulse of the doctrinaire liberal is to sweep away these barriers to reform.

But human nature also is annoyingly old-fangled; and when the usages and the constitutional provisions that have sheltered order and justice and freedom among us these three centuries are disregarded, all sorts of disagreeable problems, scarcely anticipated by the liberal doctrinaire, spring up among us. The problem of fixing responsibility in the giant union; the problem of fixing responsibility in the giant corporation; the problem of reconciling "civil rights" reform with much larger questions of constitutional structure; the difficulty of reconciling planning on a grand scale with the fallibility of any single human intellect—these, and many more such conundrums, are closely related to the human appetite for power and to the conservative principle that it is better not to do a thing at all than to do it by means which may imperil the whole complex civil social order. Order, justice, and freedom are not products of nature; on the contrary, they are most artificial and elaborate human contrivances, developed slowly and painfully out of the experience of many generations of men and women. Order, justice, and freedom cannot abide the general release of power from its ancient shackles. It may be hard to have at one's elbow the energy that could make the world anew and not to use it; but it is harder still, that power released, to restore the tolerable balance of influences which we call a free society. . . .

Part Three

OTHER DIRECTIONS: RACE, THE ARTS, AND EDUCATION

Chapter 10 MONTGOMERY AND THE QUEST FOR NEGRO RIGHTS

In 1955, MARTIN LUTHER KING, JR.
*(1929-1968), a young Baptist clergyman, helped to
organize the politically momentous Montgomery bus
boycott, which he describes in* Stride Toward
Freedom: The Montgomery Story *(1958).
Subsequently he founded and served as president of
the Southern Christian Leadership Conference,
gaining international prominence and the Nobel Peace
Prize in 1964 for his work on behalf of equal rights
for Black Americans. In 1968 his tragic assassination
shocked the nation and set off violent riots in several
cities. Eloquent spokesman during his life for a
people who were only beginning to experience the
social and economic transformations of postwar
urban America described earlier in this volume,
Reverend King was a devout Christian, champion of
integration, and unwavering advocate of peace among
men.*

. . . . On December 1, 1955, an attractive Negro seamstress, Mrs. Rosa Parks, boarded the Cleveland Avenue Bus in downtown Montgomery. She was returning home after her regular day's work in the Montgomery Fair—a leading department store. Tired from long hours on her feet, Mrs. Parks sat down in the first seat behind the section reserved for whites. Not long after she took her seat, the bus operator ordered her, along with three other Negro passengers, to move back in order to accommodate boarding white passengers. By this time every seat in the bus was taken. This meant that if Mrs. Parks followed the driver's command she would have to stand while a white male passenger, who had just boarded the bus, would sit. The other three Negro passengers immediately complied with the driver's request. But Mrs. Parks quietly refused. The result was her arrest.

Martin Luther King, Jr., *Stride Toward Freedom: The Montgomery Story* (New York: Harper & Brothers, 1958), 43-48, 159-160, 220-221. Reprinted by permission of Harper & Row, Publishers, Inc.

There was to be much speculation about why Mrs. Parks did not obey the driver. Many people in the white community argued that she had been "planted" by the NAACP in order to lay the groundwork for a test case, and at first glance that explanation seemed plausible, since she was a former secretary of the local branch of the NAACP. So persistant and persuasive was this argument that it convinced many reporters from all over the country. Later on, when I was having for human dignity and freedom. She was not "planted" there by the NAACP, or any other organization; she was planted there by her personal sense of dignity and self-respect. She was anchored to that seat by the accumulated indignities of days gone from all over the world—the invariable first question was: "Did the NAACP start the bus boycott?"

But the accusation was totally unwarranted, as the testimony of both Mrs. Parks and the officials of the NAACP revealed. Actually, no one can understand the action of Mrs. Parks unless he realizes that eventually the cup of endurance runs over, and the human personality cries out, "I can take it no longer." Mrs. Parks's refusal to move back was her intrepid affirmation that she had had enough. It was an individual expression of a timeless longing for human dignity and freedom. She was not "planted" there by the NAACP, or any other organization; she was planted there by her personal sense of dignity and self-respect. She was anchored to that seat by the accumulated indignities of days gone by and the boundless aspirations of generations yet unborn. She was a victim of both the forces of history and the forces of destiny. She had been tracked down by the *Zeitgeist*—the spirit of the time.

Fortunately, Mrs. Parks was ideal for the role assigned to her by history. She was a charming person with a radiant personality, soft spoken and calm in all situations. Her character was impeccable and her dedication deep-rooted. All of these traits together made her one of the most respected people in the Negro community.

Only E. D. Nixon—the signer of Mrs. Parks's bond—and one or two other persons were aware of the arrest when it occurred early Thursday evening. Later in the evening the word got around to a few influential women of the community, mostly members of the Women's Political Council. After a series of telephone calls back and forth they agreed that the Negroes should boycott the buses. They immediately suggested the idea to Nixon, and he readily concurred. In his usual courageous manner he agreed to spearhead the idea.

Early Friday morning, December 2, Nixon called me. He was so caught up in what he was about to say that he forgot to greet me with the usual "hello" but plunged immediately into the story of what had happened to Mrs. Parks the night before. I listened, deeply shocked, as he described the humiliating incident. "We have taken this type of thing too long already," Nixon concluded, his voice trembling. "I feel that the time has come to boycott the buses. Only through a boycott can we make it clear to the white folks that we will not accept this type of treatment any longer."

I agreed at once that some protest was necessary, and that the boycott method would be an effective one.

Just before calling me Nixon had discussed the idea with Rev. Ralph Abernathy, the young minister of Montgomery's First Baptist Church who was to become one of the central figures in the protest, and one of my closest associates. Abernathy also felt a bus boycott was our best course of action. So for thirty or forty minutes the three of us telephoned back and forth concerning plans and strategy. Nixon suggested that we call a meeting of all the ministers and civic leaders the same evening in order to get their thinking on the proposal, and I offered my church as the meeting place. The three of us got busy immediately. With the sanction of Rev. H. H. Hubbard—president of the Baptist Ministerial Alliance—Abernathy and I began calling all of the Baptist ministers. Since most of the Methodist ministers were attending a denominational meeting in one of the local churches that afternoon, it was possible for Abernathy to get the announcement to all of them simultaneously. Nixon reached Mrs. A. W. West—the widow of a prominent dentist—and enlisted her assistance in getting word to the civic leaders.

By early afternoon the arrest of Mrs. Parks was becoming public knowledge. Word of it spread around the community like uncontrolled fire. Telephones began to ring in almost rhythmic succession. By two o'clock an enthusiastic group had mimeographed leaflets concerning the arrest and the proposed boycott, and by evening these had been widely circulated.

As the hour for the evening meeting arrived, I approached the doors of the church with some apprehension, wondering how many of the leaders would respond to our call. Fortunately, it was one of those pleasant winter nights of unseasonable warmth, and to our relief, almost everybody who had been invited was on hand. More than forty people, from every segment of Negro life, were crowded into the large church meeting room. I saw physicians, schoolteachers, lawyers, businessmen, postal workers, union leaders, and clergymen. Virtually every organization of the Negro community was represented.

The largest number there was from the Christian ministry. Having left so many civic meetings in the past sadly disappointed by the dearth of ministers participating, I was filled with joy when I entered the church and found so many of them there; for then I knew that something unusual was about to happen.

Had E. D. Nixon been present, he would probably have been automatically selected to preside, but he had had to leave town earlier in the afternoon for his regular run on the railroad. In his absence, we concluded that Rev. L. Roy Bennett—as president of the Interdenominational Ministerial Alliance—was the logical person to take the chair. He agreed and was seated, his tall, erect figure dominating the room.

The meeting opened around seven-thirty with H. H. Hubbard leading a brief devotional period. Then Bennett moved into action, explaining the purpose of the gathering. With excited gestures he reported on Mrs. Parks's resistance and her arrest. He presented the proposal that the Negro citizens of Montgomery should boycott the buses on Monday in protest. "Now is the time to move," he concluded. "This is no time to talk; it is time to act."

So seriously did Bennett take his "no time to talk" admonition that for quite a while he refused to allow anyone to make a suggestion or even raise a question, insisting that we should move on and appoint committees to implement the proposal. This approach aroused the opposition of most of those present, and created a temporary uproar. For almost forty-five minutes the confusion persisted. Voices rose high, and many people threatened to leave if they could not raise questions and offer suggestions. It looked for a time as though the movement had come to an end before it began. But finally, in the face of this blistering protest, Bennett agreed to open the meeting to discussion.

Immediately questions began to spring up from the floor. Several people wanted further clarification of Mrs. Parks's actions and arrest. Then came the more practical questions. How long would the protest last? How would the idea be further disseminated throughout the community? How would the people be transported to and from their jobs?

As we listened to the lively discussion, we were heartened to notice that, despite the lack of coherence in the meeting, not once did anyone question the validity or desirability of the boycott itself. It seemed to be the unanimous sense of the group that the boycott should take place.

The ministers endorsed the plan with enthusiasm, and promised to go to their congregations on Sunday morning and drive home their approval of the projected one-day protest. Their co-öperation was significant, since virtually all of the influential Negro ministers of the city were present. It was decided that we should hold a city-wide mass meeting on Monday night, December 5, to determine how long we would abstain from riding the buses. Rev. A. W. Wilson—minister of the Holt Street Baptist Church—offered his church, which was ideal as a meeting place because of its size and central location. The group agreed that additional leaflets should be distributed on Saturday, and the chairman appointed a committee, including myself, to prepare the statement.

Our committee went to work while the meeting was still in progress. The final message was shorter than the one that had appeared on the first leaflets, but the substance was the same. It read as follows:

Don't ride the bus to work, to town, to school, or any place on Monday, December 5.

Another Negro woman has been arrested and put in jail because she refused to give up her bus seat.

Don't ride the buses to work, to town, to school, or anywhere on Monday. If you work, take a cab, or share a ride, or walk.

Come to a mass meeting, Monday at 7:00 P.M., at the Holt Street Baptist Church for further information.

After finishing the statement the committee began to mimeograph it on the church machine; but since it was late, I volunteered to have the job completed early Saturday morning.

The final question before the meeting concerned transportation. It was agreed that we should try to get the Negro taxi companies of the city—eighteen in number, with approximately 210 taxis—to transport the people for the same price that they were currently paying on the bus. A committee was appointed to make this contact, with Rev. W. J. Powell, minister of the Old Ship A.M.E. Zion Church, as chairman.

With these responsiblities before us the meeting closed. We left with our hearts caught up in a great idea. The hours were moving fast. The clock on the wall read almost midnight, but the clock in our souls revealed that it was daybreak. . . .

Ed. note: The Montgomery bus boycott which began on December 5, 1955, lasted for over eleven months, despite continuous pressure from white civic leaders and an extremist bombing of Reverend King's home. On November 13, 1956, the boycott leaders faced legal action.

Tuesday morning found us in court, once again before Judge Carter. The city's petition was directed against the MIA and several churches and individuals. It asked the court to grant the city compensation for damages growing out of the car pool operation. The city contended that it had lost more than $15,000 as a result of the reduction in bus travel (the city receives 2 per cent of the bus company revenues). It further alleged that the car pool was a "public nuisance" and a "private enterprise" operating without license fee or franchise. As the arguments unfolded the issue boiled down to this: Was the car pool a "private enterprise" operating without a franchise? Or was it a voluntary "share-a-ride" plan provided as a service by Negro churches without a profit?

As chief defendant I sat at the front table with the prosecuting and defense attorneys. Around twelve o'clock—during a brief recess—I noticed unusual commotion in the courtroom. Both Commissioner Sellers and Mayor Gayle were called to a back room, followed by two of the city attorneys. Several reporters moved excitedly in and out of the room.

I turned to Fred Gray and Peter Hall and said: "Something is wrong."

Before I could fully get these words out, Rex Thomas—a reporter for the Associated Press—came up to me with a paper in his hand.

"Here is the decision that you have been waiting for. Read this release."

Quickly, with a mixture of anxiety and hope, I read these words: "The United States Supreme Court today affirmed a decision of a special three-judge U. S. District Court in declaring Alabama's state and local laws requiring segregation on buses unconstitutional. The Supreme Court acted without listening to any argument; it simply said 'the motion to affirm is granted and the Judgment is affirmed.'"

At this moment my heart began to throb with an inexpressible joy. The darkest hour of our struggle had indeed proved to be the first hour of victory. At once I told the news to the attorneys at the table. Then I rushed to the back of the room to tell my wife, Ralph Abernathy, and E. D. Nixon. Soon the word had spread to the whole courtroom. The faces of the Negroes showed that they had heard. "God Almighty has spoken from Washington, D.C.," said one joyful bystander.

After a few minutes Judge Carter called the court to order again, and we settled down to the case at hand for the remainder of the day. About five o'clock both sides rested, and the judge's decision came in a matter of minutes: As we had all expected, the city was granted a temporary injunction to halt the motor pool. But the decision was an anticlimax. Tuesday, November 13, 1956, will always remain an important and ironic date in the history of the Montgomery bus protest. On that day two historic decisions were rendered—one to do away with the pool; the other to remove the underlying conditions that made it necessary. . . .

It is becoming clear that the Negro is in for a season of suffering. As victories for civil rights mount in the federal courts, angry passions and deep prejudices are further aroused. The mountain of state and local segregation laws still stands. Negro leaders continue to be arrested and harassed under city ordinances, and their homes continue to be bombed. State laws continue to be enacted to circumvent integration. I pray that, recognizing the necessity of suffering, the Negro will make of it a virtue. To suffer in a righteous cause is to grow to our humanity's full stature. If only to save himself from bitterness, the Negro needs the vision to see the ordeals of this generation as the opportunity to transfigure himself and American society. If he has to go to jail for the cause of freedom, let him enter it in the fashion Gandhi urged his countrymen, "as the bridegroom enters the bride's chamber"— that is, with a little trepidation but with great expectation.

Nonviolence is a way of humility and self-restraint. We Negroes talk a great deal about our rights, and rightly so. We proudly proclaim that three-fourths of the poeple of the world are colored. We have the privilege of watching in our generation the great drama of freedom and independence as it unfolds in Asia and Africa. All of these things are in line with the work of providence. We must be sure, however, that we accept them in the right spirit. In an effort to achieve freedom in America, Asia, and Africa we must not try to leap from a position of disadvantage to one of advantage, thus subverting justice. We must seek democracy and not the substitution of one tyranny for another. Our aim must never be to defeat or humiliate the white man. We must not become victimized with a philosophy of black supremacy. God is not interested merely in the freedom of black men, and brown men, and yellow men; God is interested in the freedom of the whole human race.

The nonviolent approach provides an answer to the long debated question of gradualism *versus* immediacy. On the one hand it prevents one from falling into the sort of patience which is an excuse for do-nothingism and escapism, ending up in standstillism. On the other hand it saves one from the irresponsible words which estrange without reconciling and the hasty judgment which is blind to the necessities of social process. It recognizes the need for moving toward the goal of justice with wise restraint and calm reasonableness. But it also recognizes the immorality of slowing up in the move toward justice and capitulating to the guardians of an unjust status quo. It recognizes that social change cannot come overnight. But it causes one to work as if it were a possibility the next morning.

Through nonviolence we avoid the temptation of taking on the psychology of victors. Thanks largely to the noble and invaluable work of the NAACP, we have won great victories in the federal courts. But we must not be self-satisfied. We must respond to every decision with an understanding of those who have opposed us, and with acceptance of the new adjustments that the court orders pose for them. We must act in such a way that our victories will be triumphs for good will in all men, white and Negro. . . .

Chapter 11 AFFLUENCE AND THE ARTS

CARL N. DEGLER (1921-   ), professor of history at Stanford University, describes clearly in these excerpts from his book, Affluence and Anxiety: 1945-Present *(1968), still other voices of the 1950's—those of artists and architects in an "age of alienation." Whether alienation can altogether be pushed back into the early 1950's is debatable, despite unmistakable signs of its emergence; but this idea is helpful as a corrective for notions of "A Silent Generation" or a gray-flannelled era. Degler, moreover, correctly stresses the displacement in the 1950's of the social concerns of depression years by interest in individual release, personal identification, and self-expression. Abstract expressionism, however, represents continuity as well as apparent dramatic change in the world of art. While the abstract expressionists shunned paintings that were merely representations of some other reality, they were doggedly pursuing realism, both in their techniques and their emphasis on the painting as the end in itself. Thus the artist literally immerses himself in his work—the harder the surface, the better—while the painting "has a life of its own." Abstract expressionism and the new, more decorative architecture were appropriate to the Eisenhower Era in other regards as well, made possible, as Degler notes, by the affluence of the age. They also found a tolerant, or insecure, and sometimes admiring audience for nonconformity. The critical and popular response to abstract expressionism was the artistic equivalent of parental and societal permissiveness in an other-directed society.*

. . . . If in many ways mass culture tends to a sameness and a level of approach that are oppressive, it has at least not insisted upon the prudishness or opposition to controversy that had characterized earlier periods in American cultural history. The movies and, to a lesser extent, television, in the 1950's and 1960's have found it possible to discuss heretofore explosive questions like the race issue (*Pinky*), religious fanaticism (*Elmer Gantry*), and sexual deviation (*Tea and Sympathy*). In 1966 when Edward Albee's violent play *Who's Afraid of Virginia Woolf?* appeared as a movie, it marked a new high in freedom of expression in language and ideas, yet it suffered no bans. Even television in the early 1960's felt bold and free enough to discuss candidly and maturely heretofore forbidden issues such as abortion and contraception. Two novels long banned from the United States because of their

Carl N. Degler, *Affluence and Anxiety: 1945-Present* (Chicago: Scott, Foresman and Company, 1968), 197-200, 205-207. Reprinted by permission.

alleged pornographic content, D. H. Lawrence's *Lady Chatterley's Lover* and Henry Miller's *Tropic of Cancer*, were both permitted to be published in 1959-1960. Perhaps the most shocking novel of artistic quality written in the 1950's, Vladimir Nabokov's best-selling *Lolita* (1959), which was later made into a movie, was subjected to no federal ban at all.

A Literature of Prosperity and Individuality. Two broad influences shaped the literature of post-1945 America. One was the boom, which removed from the center of the stage the social themes of the literature of the 1930's. Writers now felt free to indulge their interest in and concern for more individual matters. And in a society increasingly affluent, many artists felt a strong desire to examine critically individual character and values.

Furthermore, the unsettled state of the post-1945 world encouraged individualistic introspection and analysis. Until the death of Stalin in 1953, the threat of nuclear war in Europe was ever present; after that date the rising power of China in Asia offered new causes for anxiety. And following 1960 the increasing American involvement in the war in Vietnam exacerbated fears of war with China, possibly leading to World War III, and the nuclear destruction of the world. Affluence and anxiety became central themes. The irony of the 1950's and 1960's was that as nations became more powerful with their rockets, hydrogen bombs, and supersonic jets, individual men seemed to shrink in power. It was almost as if with each scientific gain in the ability to destroy, men felt less and less able to effect changes either in their own highly organized and complex society or in the world at large. Man may have been gaining ever greater mastery over nature, but individual men felt more helpless than ever.

This awareness of the alienation of man from himself and from the mass production society that he has created runs through much of the literature of the time. Indeed, alienation—the feeling that man is a stranger to himself—is a central theme in European as well as American culture. Existentialist philosophy, emphasizing the individual's total responsibility for his own acts, even in a universe viewed as absurd, became almost a fad in intellectual circles in Europe and America soon after 1945. Albert Camus, the great French novelist of the period, became the high priest of cultural existentialism after the publication of *The Stranger* (1946) and *The Plague* (1948). Camus' novels were widely read on college campuses, and for a while in the 1950's, he was an intellectual hero of many American college students.

The most noticeable effect of the new prosperity on American writing was the abandonment of social concern and criticism. There was still, to be sure, rebellion against society in postwar novels, but the dissatisfaction was not directed against specific injustices as in Steinbeck's *Grapes of Wrath* or the proletarian writings of the 1930's. In fact, few of the novels of the 1950's and 1960's were problem novels, as Sinclair Lewis' *Main Street* or John Dos Passos' *U.S.A.* were, though the naturalism of these earlier works is still clearly in evidence. Norman Mailer's *The Naked and the Dead* (1948), one of the best of the novels about World War II, and

Saul Bellow's *The Adventures of Augie March* (1953), for example, are cast in the naturalistic mold that had begun to be in evidence in the 1890's and which had shaped the fiction of the 1920's and 1930's. The focus of the naturalistic novel after the war, however, is not society itself, but the place of the individual within society. For that reason, some critics see the inspiration of these postwar writers as coming from the giants of the nineteenth century—Melville and Twain, for example —rather than from the more recent and strictly naturalistic writers like Dreiser, Dos Passos, and Sinclair Lewis.

Because many writers feel acutely the loss of identity in a highly organized, gigantic mass society that threatens to overwhelm them, they emphasize the individual. Critic Ihab Hassan, writing on the literature of the 1950's, characterizes the hero of the novels of the period as being both rebel and victim. The hero typically rebels against organization and society while at the same time he is also a victim of the state and technology. Simply because the protagonists (they are drawn on too small a scale to be called heroes) in these novels are aware of their slightness, the emphasis is placed upon their identity or their search for identity. The purpose in many of these novels is to find existential fulfillment—that is, freedom and self-definition. The important thing is action, for in doing something the individual defines himself by differentiating himself from the mass. Resistance against authority or rebellion is the surest way of asserting one's humanity. As Albert Camus summed it up, "I rebel—therefore we exist." Only in the assertion of self against society can a man's humanity be recognized. Another critic, R. W. B. Lewis, saw the principal novelists of the period as being united on "the subject of self—of acquiring a clear sense of the self or of charging on against fearful odds to an integral self already in being." Manifestations of this same philosophy will be seen later in this chapter in the action painting of Jackson Pollock and Willem de Kooning and in the commitment of many college students to civil rights action and protests against the Vietnam War.

The concern with individual identity can be observed in a number of the major novels of the period. In James Jones' *From Here to Eternity* (1951), Private Prewitt seeks to maintain his individuality in the prewar army. He likes the army life, even though he cannot express himself freely. Yet he will not meekly accept either. Hence he is both a rebel and a victim. He rebels against the organization itself, but he does not rebel against the system that created it, unlike what so often happened in the social novels of the 1930's. He stands as a symbol of antipower in an organization (the Army) and in a society, the powers of which are overwhelmingly stronger than that of any individual. Even in a relatively minor novel like Mary McCarthy's *The Group* (1963), the concern for individuality is clear. Although the novel ostensibly takes place in the socially concerned thirties, it is striking that the book itself deals with the struggles of eight young women for self-hood and individual identification.

William Styron's powerful *Lie Down in Darkness* (1951) depicts the deteriorating relationship between a girl and her father in the stifling atmosphere of a small southern town. Each is searching for his own identity as well as for an enduring relationship with the other. The failure of the search ends in suicide for one and a chronic alcoholism for the other. Even more clearly manifest is the search for identity in two novels by Saul Bellow, one of the most significant writers of the postwar years. In *Henderson the Rain King* (1959) the question of identity is only lightly disguised by fantasy and in *Herzog* (1964) it is not hidden at all. Bernard Malamud's *A New Life* (1961), though comic in form, is clearly pursuing the theme of identity, both in the title and in the story of the inadequate college instructor who seeks his identity by changing his environment.

J. D. Salinger is one of the most popular and highly regarded writers of the period. His first book, *Catcher in the Rye* (1951) portrays the inner rebellion of the adolescent youth in his own language by chronicling the struggle of Holden Caulfield for identification and self-awareness. Salinger continues his exploration of the youthful search for self in his later work about college age youths, *Franny and Zooey* (1961).

An Exception. It is true that generally the period after 1945 witnessed the rapid decline of the socially conscious novel, but novels by Negro writers, it needs to be added, constitute an important exception to this generalization. In a way, Negro writers only came into their own after the Depression, and even then, as a people. Negroes were still dominated by the discrimination and poverty which they experienced even in the prosperous fifties. Hence it is not surprising that there continues to be a deep social anger in the writings of James Baldwin and Ralph Ellison. (One of the reasons for the wider appreciation of Negro writers since the Depression was that prosperity brought forth a new and growing Negro book-reading public.) Probably the most highly regarded novel by a Negro is Ralph Ellison's *The Invisible Man* (1952), which convincingly and relentlessly portrays the frustrations and dangers of being a black man in white America. Undoubtedly the best-known Negro writer of the 1950's and 1960's is James Baldwin, an erstwhile protégé of the outstanding Negro novelist of the 1930's, Richard Wright, and, like Wright, for a time an expatriate in Paris. In his first novel, *Go Tell It on the Mountain* (1953), Baldwin wrote about the great Negro migration from the South to the urban slums of the North, but the book's point of view is essentially devoid of social criticism. As the Negro revolution boiled up, however, Baldwin, in his nonfiction writings, notably *Notes of a Native Son* (1955), *Nobody Knows My Name* (1961), and *The Fire Next Time* (1963), was revealed as an unusually articulate and powerful spokesman for the militant Negro in his drive for equality. Not surprisingly, Baldwin's fiction became increasingly imbued with his social concerns. Thus his ambitious, but only moderately successful, novel *Another Country* (1962) is given over almost entirely to a frontal assault on both sexual and racial conventions. . . .

As in literature, social concerns became muted in painting as prosperity replaced depression. A few well-known, socially committed artists like Ben Shahn continued to concern themselves in the 1950's with social themes, representationally presented. As Shahn said in connection with his "Miners' Wives," he assumed, "that most people are interested in the hopes, fears, and dreams and tragedies of other people, for those are the things that life is made of." But Shahn's social interests, like his representational style, were clearly a minority approach in the 1950's and after. Abstractionism has held the center of the artistic stage. Simply because abstract works deny to themselves the traditional symbols of visual communication, they fitted into the new individualism and freedom of the 1950's. Painting became individually expressive rather than socially communicative.

Two of the best representatives of the new American school of abstract expressionism are Jackson Pollock and Willem de Kooning. Both men consciously broke with the social concerns of the 1930's, picking up where the great European abstractionists had left off when the war began. As De Kooning later said, "Jackson Pollock broke the ice." Even in the 1940's Pollock shunned representation in his paintings. This complete rejection of representational art admirably represents the dominant trend in modern art. For today, more than at any other period, art is a means of self-release and self-discovery, almost a substitute for religion. It is keyed to the individual artist, not to society. The absence of the traditional symbols of visual communication make it unavoidably individualistic. Each painting is a distinctly individual statement by the artist, removing any need even for titles and, in fact, there often are none. At a time when men fear being lost in a mass society, or being destroyed by nuclear war, the artistic accent is upon originality and uniqueness.

When Pollock talked about his method of painting, the emphasis upon individuality was clear in his deliberate departure from convention and in his desire to be *in* the painting, thereby making it fully his. "My painting does not come from the easel," he said. "I hardly ever stretch my canvas before painting. I prefer to tack the unstretched canvas to the hard wall or the floor. I need the resistance of hard surface. On the floor I am more at ease. I feel nearer, more part of the painting, since this way I can walk around it, work from the four sides and literally be *in* the painting. . . .

"I continued to get further away from the usual painter's tools such as easel, palette, brushes, etc. I prefer sticks, trowels, knives, and dripping fluid paint or a heavy impasto [thickly laid paint] with sand, broken glass and other foreign matter added.

"When I am *in* my painting, I'm not aware of what I'm doing. It is only after a sort of 'get acquainted' period that I see what I have been about. I have no fears about making changes, destroying the image, etc., because the painting has a life of its own. I try to let it come through. It is only when I lose contact with the painting that the result is a mess. Otherwise there is pure harmony, and easy give and take and the painting comes out well."

Typical of Pollock's many paintings is "Blue Poles" (1953), which makes only a vague concession to representation in the eight slanting lines (poles?) that dominate the canvas. Using silvery aluminum paint along with brilliant red, yellow, and orange as well as cool blue, the huge painting overwhelms the viewer. To some critics the purpose of this and other works of abstract expressionism is to convey the intensity of the artist's personal reaction to an affluent and complex society composed of big organizations, where he is constantly oppressed by the anxiety resulting from the ever present threat of nuclear destruction. Pollock conveys the force of his feeling largely through brilliant color; in De Kooning's works after 1954, the same feeling is often portrayed in bold and powerful strokes in broad slashes of paint. The assertion of individuality is also symbolized in the enormous size of the canvases. ("Blue Poles," for example, is 7 feet by 16 feet, or about the size of a wall of a large room.) The very size of the pictures fairly shouts for attention. In fact, the size of the giant canvases, often as large as a traditional mural, has become the hallmark of the new American abstract expressionism.

Willem de Kooning made his entrance into the front rank of international, as well as American, modern art with a remarkable series of six painting, collectively entitled "The Women." The story of the creation of "Woman I" (1953) exemplifies the extremely individualistic attitude of contemporary art. De Kooning worked for years on "Woman I," changing it, scraping off pounds of paint, hurling more pounds upon the canvas with almost demonic energy, all the while anxiously scrutinizing it by day and by night. Then, in a fit of despair over getting it right, he hurled the paint-laden canvas into a corner, disgusted. Later, after reconsideration, he attacked the job once again, bringing it to completion and public view. The word "attack" is accurate, for the painting is a battleground of his own emotions; the result is the carnage left by the struggle to express himself fully. In the end the vaguely hateful woman who emerged on the canvas symbolizes art itself, still triumphant in the age of the machine. It is clear that the justification of the painting is De Kooning's own individual expression and nothing else. As he himself said, "Painting is a way of living. . . . That is where the form of it lies."

De Kooning's work fits into this age of alienation in still another fashion. His paintings depict what one critic has called "no-environment"—that is, they are made up of anything at hand, a scrap of this, a piece of that. The resulting paintings are thus nothing and yet everything. They are all pieces of the real world, but jumbled together in such a way that no single place and yet every place is suggested. And perhaps that is how it feels to be an alienated man; he has no place and is therefore at home everywhere; he is no one and yet is everyone.

At one time during the long years of his early obscurity, De Kooning concluded that the artist has no place in the modern world, especially in America. But the subsequent recognition accorded him as an important artist has belied that view. By realizing himself in his paintings, without compromise, without truckling to popular tastes, he has triumphed both as a person and as an artist. For him, as for modern art in general, this achievement signals the triumph of the individual. . . .

Chapter 12 THE CRITIQUE OF PROGRESSIVE EDUCATION

*Progressive educators concerned about "real-life experiences"
and "the whole child" exercised a commanding influence
on the curricula and organization of American schools for
over three decades following the First World War. A
reaction against progressive education occurred in the
1950's, with a torrent of articles and books criticizing the
elementary schools for failing to teach skills of reading and
writing, the high schools for stressing "life-adjustment
education," and the teachers' colleges for having created
the "crisis of education." Perhaps the most influential of
the critics of progressive education was ARTHUR E. BESTOR
(1908-   ), a university historian who wrote and spoke
extensively on the need for attention to basic academic
disciplines, scholarship in teaching, and the ability to think.
The following passages are taken from Bestor's book,* Educational Wastelands *(1953), which was revised as* The Restoration
of Learning *(1955). The arguments of the Eisenhower Era on
behalf of educational excellence were a crucial element in
turning the attention of the nation toward the schools and
colleges and making possible their impressive improvement
following the Soviet Union's launching of the orbiting Sputnik
in 1957. These developments occurred in a time of national
concern, unity of purpose, interest in new departures, and
simultaneous concensus on many basic values.*

. . . . What kind of training should the schools offer if they are to endow future citizens with the disciplined intellectual powers that we have been discussing? This question is at once the most important and the most difficult that can be asked in the realm of educational theory. It is far wider in scope and far more profound than the question, What methods of instruction should be used? Persons who are trained to deal with the latter question, the question of pedagogy, do not necessarily possess any particular qualifications for dealing with the former, the question of the curriculum. No single group of specialists, in fact, can claim special competence in the matter. The idea that there can be a "curriculum expert" is as absurd as the idea that there can be an expert on the meaning of life. . . .

Arthur E. Bestor, *Educational Wastelands: The Retreat from Learning in Our Public Schools* (Urbana: The University of Illinois Press, 1953), pp. 40, 43-47, 54-55, 59-60. Reprinted by permission. Footnotes omitted.

By accepting the unfounded pretensions of so-called professors of education, we have permitted the content of public school instruction to be determined by a narrow group of specialists in pedagogy, well-intentioned men and women, no doubt, but utterly devoid of the qualifications necessary for the task they have undertaken. These pedagogical experts are making decisions that involve considerations far outside the realm of pedagogy. They are deciding not merely *how* subjects should be taught in the public schools, but also *what* subjects should be taught. Under the guise of improving the *methods* of instruction, they have undertaken to determine its *content* as well. They are usurping a function that belongs to the learned world as a whole. It is the entire body of scholars, scientists, and professional men, not one particular group among them, who possess collectively the expert knowledge that should be applied to curriculum-making. They are the men and women who know the kinds of intellectual skills that are vitally necessary to maintain the life of the nation in flourishing condition, for they are the ones who are actively engaged in advancing knowledge and applying it to the practical problems of the present-day world. They are the ones who ought to be advising the people concerning the content of the public school curriculum, in order that the people's decisions may be wise ones.

As a result of the intrusion of the pedagogues into curriculum-making, the schools are being more and more completely divorced from the basic disciplines of science and learning. Intellectual training, once the unquestioned focus of every educational effort, has been pushed out to the periphery of the public school program. Into the vacuum have rushed the "experts" from state departments and colleges of education: the curriculum doctors, the integrators, the life-adjusters—the specialists in know-how rather than knowledge. Out of their overflowing minds they offer to furnish ready-made a philosophy to guide the entire educational system. All that scientists and scholars need do is supply little facts to fill up the blanks in the great schemata which the educationists devise. The curriculum engineers will do the rest. They will be happy to draw the really vital generalizations from the data which grubbers in laboratories and libraries so obligingly but so uninspiredly amass. They will point out to the teachers (unimaginative dullards, as they see them) the relationships that exist among the great fields of knowledge. That a discipline may have order, logic, and proportion within itself is a fact that seems to have escaped their notice. Is it any wonder that the curricula of many American public schools today are so trivial, so unbalanced, so out of harmony with the thinking of trained scientists and scholars that they constitute a mere parody of education?

In the discussion thus far I have not used the term "progressive education." I have deliberately refrained from doing so, because the phrase is vague and ambiguous. It is applied to a multitude of different programs, with many of which I am in hearty sympathy. On the other hand, many tendencies in contemporary American education that are labelled progressive can be more accurately described, I believe, as "regressive education."

So long as students of pedagogy recognized the inherent limitations of what they were doing, they made important contributions to the improvement of public education. Through careful study of child psychology and through controlled experimentation in the classroom, they pointed the way to notable advances in the technique of imparting such elementary skills as reading and arithmetic; they increased the effectiveness with which such high school subjects as history, chemistry, algebra, and foreign languages were taught; and they succeeded in so increasing the efficiency of instruction that students were prepared to undertake in the high school certain studies usually considered as belonging to the college program. In the early part of the present century these improved methods of instruction went by the name of progressive education. For that type of progressive education I have sincere respect. If professional educationists had concentrated their efforts upon putting these improvements into effect throughout the schools, instead of turning aside from their proper work to tamper with the curriculum itself, then educational progress over the past half century would have been an unquestionable fact.

Educational progress *was* a fact so long as progressive education meant things I have just described. I consider myself fortunate to have received my high school training, from 1922 to 1926, in one of the most progressive schools in the country, the Lincoln School of Teachers College, Columbia University. In those years, and in that school, progressive education seems to me to have been definitely on the right track. With uninfluential exceptions the faculty of that school did not think of defining the aims of secondary education apart from the aims of liberal education generally. They believed thoroughly in the educational purposes that had always been central in education as a whole. They knew that the work of the secondary school must intermesh with the advanced work carried on by scientists and scholars. Adequate preparation for college was not a separate goal; it was the natural consequence of a sound secondary school program based on the great intellectual disciplines. Mathematical instruction in the Lincoln School culminated in a senior course in the calculus, a branch of mathematics ordinarily commenced only in college. A full year was devoted to each of the sciences of chemistry, physics, and biology. The classical languages, it is true, were sacrificed to modernity—a serious mistake, I believe—but the promise that they would be replaced by sound training in the living foreign languages was honestly fulfilled. Work in English included the study of contemporary authors, but with no slighting of the great literature of the past. Composition meant a study of grammar and syntax, and in addition the practice of original writing of the sort published in Mr. Hughes Mearn's admirable *Creative Youth*.

What progressive educationists undertook to do, in those fruitful years, was to bring the teaching of the basic disciplines to the highest perfection possible in the light of modern pedagogy. They did so by emphasizing the relevance of knowledge and intellectual skill to the problems of practical life and citizenship. They experimented with more effective methods of instruction, and they never forgot that the good faith of an experimenter is measured by his frankness in conceding the failure. Above all, they sought the ablest teachers, not the ones most fanatically devoted to newness for its own sake. The success of the Lincoln School in attracting brilliant men and women to its faculty was remarkable. To several of my teachers there I owe as much as to any of my instructors in college and graduate school, and I am proud to say that I am in correspondence with at least two of them more than a quarter of a century later.

Yet the shadow of the future began to fall upon the Lincoln School even in the middle twenties. Alongside excellent instruction in history, a course in the "social studies" was introduced. Subsequent work of my own in several of the fields supposedly embraced within this course has merely confirmed the opinion which my classmates and I entertained at the time. I remember being struck at the outset by the inferiority of this hodgepodge to the straightforward treatment of great public issues that I had learned to expect from my instructors in history. The "social studies" purported to throw light on contemporary problems, but the course signally failed, for it offered no perspective on the issues it raised, no basis for careful analysis, no encouragement to ordered thinking. There was plenty of discussion, but it was hardly responsible discussion. Quick and superficial opinions, not balanced and critical judgment, were at a premium. Freedom to think was elbowed aside by freedom not to think, and undisguised indoctrination loomed ahead. I am surprised at how accurately we as students appraised the course. I cannot now improve on the nickname we gave it at the time: "social stew."

The course in the social studies, and the more destructive programs that ensued, marked a turning point in progressive education. The label remained the same, but the thing itself became appallingly different. Progressive education ceased to be an effort to accomplish more effectively the purposes which citizens, scholars, and scientists had agreed were fundamental. Progressive education began to imply the substitution of new purposes. Experts in pedagogy were feeling their oats, were abandoning their proper task of improving instruction, and were brazenly undertaking to redefine the aims of education itself. By disregarding or flatly rejecting the considered educational views of the scholarly, scientific, and professional world, these new educationists succeeded in converting the division between secondary and higher education from a mere organizational fact into a momentous intellectual schism. Progressive education became regressive education, because, instead of advancing, it began to undermine the great traditions of liberal education and to substitute for them lesser aims, confused aims, or no aims at all.

Regressive education is the direct consequence of the fact that public school educationists have severed all real connection with the great world of science and learning. The only test of a public school program today is whether it is good in the eyes of an expert in pedagogy; whether it is sound in the eyes of a scholar in the field is a question that is no longer asked. Regressive education, in fact, is simply the mind of the typical professor of pedagogy writ large. That mind has its virtues, and those virtues appeared in the genuine progressive education of a generation ago, for enlightened pedagogy was then applied to the realization of aims in which all educated men concurred. But the pedagogic mind has its grave limitations also, and these have come to the fore in proportion as scholarly and scientific influence over educational policy has weakened. Most men's intellectual defects, of course, are counterparts of their virtues. A good quality is corrupted into a vice by being carried to excess. This is largely true of the situation I am describing. The interests and preoccupations of the pedagogical expert, praiseworthy when controlled and directed, have received so abnormal an emphasis in contemporary school programs as to be destructive of the very purposes of the school. . . .

The attempt to by-pass essential stages in the process of learning to use the mind is characteristic of regressive education. Most present-day proposals with respect to the public school curriculum bristle with pious words about teaching children to think. Upon careful analysis, however, an appalling number of them depend upon finding some short-cut to intellectual discipline. Their authors seem to believe—against all reason and experience—that it is possible to train men to perform the culminating acts of thought, while skipping all the antecedent steps.

Now effective thinking, I would suggest, involves at least four things. In the first place, it requires a thorough command of the essential intellectual tools. The most important of these would certainly be the ability to read, by which I mean the power to grasp the full meaning of the printed page, no matter how difficult, and in which I would include the ability to read more than a single language. Almost equal in importance would be the ability to write, which is not just the ability to make decipherable marks on paper, but the ability to put complex ideas into intelligible prose and to handle the niceties of syntax with the assurance born of grammatical analysis. Some command of mathematical thinking, beyond the mechanical processes of arithmetic, is also requisite to thinking, certainly for this present age in which quantified data are so significant.

In the second place, effective thinking depends upon a store of reliable information, which the mind can draw upon. It is commonly said that men do not need to carry information in their minds, because they can look it up in reference books. Every man, of course, no matter how well educated, must look up many items of information in connection with every enterprise he engages in. But in order to do so, he has to possess a great deal of information to begin with. A reference book merely explains one thing in terms of another. The user can pursue a chain of cross references, of course, but eventually he must trace a connection to something he already knows, else the pursuit is an utterly meaningless one. A man must bring to any reference book a fund of ready knowledge sufficient to make it intelligible.

In the third place, effective intellectual effort presupposes long-continued practice in the systematic ways of thinking developed within the various basic fields of scholarly and scientific investigation. To approach a new problem from the point of view of its historical origins involves much more than a knowledge of certain facts of history. One must have already thought through other problems of historical causation, and one must have become aware of the pitfalls that exist in the interpretation of historical data. A man needs to know the inner structure and logic of any system of thought if he is to use its resources to any serious purpose.

Finally, but only finally, comes the culminating act of applying this aggregate of intellectual powers to the solution of a problem. In a sense, perhaps, this is the only step which can properly be called thinking. But it is not a step that can be taken by itself; it presupposes the preceding steps. And one cannot teach men to think by training them to perform this final act alone, any more than one can build a house from the roof downwards. . . .

The disciplined mind is what education at every level should strive to produce. It is important for the individual. It is even more important for society. It is most important of all for a democratic society. In that terrifying novel of George Orwell, *1984*, the Party of Big Brother developed the ultimate in ruthless dictatorship precisely because it devised the means of enslaving men's minds. It began by undermining the discipline of history, setting all men adrift in a world where past experience became meaningless. It continued by undermining the discipline of language, debasing speech until it could no longer be the vehicle of independent thought. And the crowning triumph of torture-chambers was the undermining of the disciplines of logic and mathematics, the forcing of its victims not only to assert, but actually to believe, that two plus two equals five.

Fortunately it is as yet only through fantasy that we can see what the destruction of the scholarly and scientific disciplines would mean to mankind. From history we can learn what their existence has meant. The sheer power of disciplined thought is revealed in practically all the great intellectual and technological advances which the human race has made. The ability of the man of disciplined mind to direct this power effectively upon problems for which he was not specifically trained is proved by instances without number. The real evidence for the value of liberal education lies, where pedagogical experimenters and questionnaire-makers refuse to seek it, in history and in the biographies of men who have met the valid criteria of greatness. These support overwhelmingly the claim of liberal education that it can equip a man or woman with fundamental powers of decision and action, applicable not merely to huckstering and housekeeping, but to all the great and varied concerns of human life—not least, those which are unforeseen. . . .

Part Four

THE EISENHOWER LEADERSHIP

Chapter 13 EISENHOWER'S PERSONALITY AND POLITICS

EMMET JOHN HUGHES *(1920-   ) worked as a speech writer for Dwight D. Eisenhower in the election campaigns of 1952 and 1956 and during the President's first year in office. Hughes had been a foreign correspondent and* Time-Life *bureau chief in Rome and Berlin, and was more recently a columnist and editorial consultant for Newsweek and the Washington* Post. *Since 1968 he has been a special assistant to Governor Nelson Rockefeller of New York. A liberal internationalist who advocated presidential leadership in public and partisan affairs, Hughes espoused "modern Republicanism" and was hostile to Vice President Richard M. Nixon and to conservatives in the Eisenhower administration. Writing during the administration of John F. Kennedy, whose active political leadership Hughes admired, he describes Ike's style with mixed feelings and decries the 1950's as a "lost decade" for the Republican party and for the nation.*

. . . . Upon first encounter, the man instantly conveyed one quality—strength. . . . there was a feature of his face impossible to ignore or to forget—the blue eyes of a force and intensity singularly deep, almost disturbing, above all commanding. They were, I would quickly learn, eyes astonishingly expressive, almost *articulate*. In the months and years to come, I would watch them moving quickly and inquisitively from face to face around the Cabinet table, staring solemnly over a hushed audience, darting impatiently from paper to paper on the immense desk in the oval office in the White House—and drooping heavily with fatigue. Always they would speak of the moment and the mood: icy with anger, warm with satisfaction, sharp with concern, glazed with boredom. And always somehow—was it their eloquent explicitness of feeling?—they conveyed an image and a sense of strength.

The physical fact symbolized a political fact. The man, throughout the campaign of 1952, seemed in firm and sure command of himself and of all around him. Nor—standing close to him—did one feel this command compromised or shaken on the few occasions when his own instinct did bow to another's urging. For when he deferred to a contrary judgment, the act seemed never to issue from weakness or meekness. It rather seemed a gladly given sign of healthy-self confidence in a man who felt no need to prove the steel of his will by mere stubbornness of opinion.

Equally . . . revealing was his distaste for direct personal critique—or, worse still, counterattack—in the political arena. In a long discussion we once had on the question, provoked by my proposing some retort to a charge by the opposition, he expanded: "I simply do not believe it does a damn bit of good wasting time answering the other fellow. All you do is double the audience he had the first time when he proclaimed whatever it is you are trying to answer." As the campaign moved toward its climactic weeks, with President Harry Truman sharpening his attacks, the private retort of Eisenhower was: "I'm sure they would like me to get down to *their* level. Well, that's one satisfaction they will *never* have." And this hot feeling of personal pride ruled his whole personal attitude toward the campaign— the sense of personal integrity so keen that it could, at times, impute *lack* of integrity to anyone guilty of failing to recognize and respect his.

One October day, he gave me an incisive little speech on the matter. "All I can hope to do in this or any other campaign," he affirmed, "is to say what I believe. And this does *not* mean always getting into wrangles and scuffles with the other fellow, to the point where the people can't any longer figure out just what we're fighting about. The people who listen to me want to know what *I* think—not what I think about what someone *else* thinks. This is all I have to offer. If the people believe in what I say and do, nothing else matters—and they will vote for me. If they don't, there's nothing I can do about it." And then came a note struck often, not only in these months but also in years to come. "If they don't want me, that doesn't matter very much to *me*. I've got a hell of a lot of fishing I'll be happy to do."

All these conversations gave early testimony to marks of character and habits of thought that would stamp themselves on so much the man would do, and refuse to do, in the years ahead. There was the stubborn search for the simple—the striving, only partly conscious and deliberate, to reduce all issues to some bare essence, starkly seen and graphically stated. From this, however, a paradox would follow. The man who so shunned all hint of the personal in political life would, by this coveting of simplification, often apply an intensely personal definition to the most historic world matters—as when, as President, he would impose the test of "sincerity" upon the conduct of the Soviet Union.

There was visible here, too, the slightly disdainful aloofness from aggressive politics; and it was hard, for example, to imagine such a man wielding the sharp-edged weapons of patronage for coldly planned effect. And there was, clear above all else, the aversion to rough political combat, especially the hurtful political thrust, that would temper so drastically his conduct toward Republican enemies as well as Democratic opponents.

Dominant in all he said . . . was an almost fiercely stubborn resolve to respect the truth as he saw it. There were times, before the campaign ended, when advisers could persuade him either to do something personally distasteful or to stifle what he most wished to say. There were times, too, when he would blurt out thoughtless phrases, unreflected and imprecise, sometimes even harsh. But it was unthinkable—and everyone near him knew it was unthinkable—that he would willfully twist a fact, distort an issue, or delude with an empty pledge.

. . . Provoked by almost any passing criticism, or lament upon his handling of the Congress, he would push back his leather chair, grimace tightly, vault upright, and start his march-to-rhetoric around the oval office. . . . "Now, look, I happen to *know* a little about leadership. I've had to work with a lot of nations, for that matter, at odds with each other. And I tell you this: you do not *lead* by hitting people over the head. Any damn fool can do that, but it's usually called 'assault'—not 'leadership.' . . .I'll tell you what leadership is. It's *persuasion*—and *conciliation*—and *education*—and *patience*. It's long, slow, tough work. That's the only kind of leadership I know or believe in—or will practice."

He would stop in his striding on such occasions, to note bitterly some suddenly remembered disparagement of his "lack of aggressiveness." And he would surge on, firing his furious words at the critical, anonymous "them." . . . "*They* talk and write and prate about leadership. And they'd be happy and cheering—if I knocked some Congressional heads together. Well, I *won't*—not even the thickest heads in my own party—not if I can possibly avoid it. For that will not be leadership, and I'll tell you *why*. In the first place, you don't 'lead' a man by yelling at him in public or forcing him to say publicly, 'Yes, it's true—I've been voting like a damn fool ever since I came to Congress twenty years ago.' In the second place, if I forced some of these fellows to go through that kind of public penance and conversion—how long do you think they would *stay* converted? I'll tell you—long enough to get off their knees, run a short distance, and curse me for humiliating them. And in the third place, when Senator X or Senator Z does something I think is just deplorable, more than half the time that means he's a Republican—*supposed* to be helping me, not working against me. So if I tell him off in public, what am I accomplishing? Just this much: I am yelling to the world, 'Please come and look, all of you, at the knuckle-head I have representing me and my party and my program on Capitol Hill.' "

And this heated declamation would end, almost invariably, on a softening note, as his voice slowly attuned and yielded to the sense of personal humility and personal responsibility.... "Look," he would almost implore, "I know how good I could make *myself* look. Everyone who's yapping now would be cheering . . . if only I would do my 'leading' in public—where they could *see* me.... Well, I can't do that. I will spend the hours here, quietly, in this office, staring out these windows, sometimes a little hopelessly—with Dirksen or Millikin or Knowland here, to tell me what industries I have to protect with higher tariffs—or how the folks back home don't like these big bills for Mutual Security—or how to put Chiang Kai-shek back in Peiping . . . So I'll listen. And I'll answer. And I'll try to get them to understand, to *give*. I'll try to get them to give not everything, but—a little here, a little there. And I'll hope that maybe something I say *does* get through—and stays with them." And finally he would end with the candid confession, murmured not meekly but firmly: "I don't know any other way to lead."

There shone in these words and perceptions—so I believed—qualities even more substantial than manifest sincerity. There was full awareness, here, of the harsh dilemma tormenting any President at deep odds, in critical areas, with some of his own party's most cherished traditions and comfortable postures. There was honorable willingness, too, to accept a formidable task, even though possibly underestimating its immensity: the direction of government and the leadership of party, while simultaneously striving to inspire this party both to renovate its structure and to renounce its prejudices. All the seeming simplicity of the President's words, in short, was deceptive, for they actually described some of the most tangled and complex political knots that can be tied by the democratic process itself.

. . . Knowland—even after succeeding Taft as Senate Majority Leader, supposedly serving as the President's key aide on the Hill—showed ponderous and determined lethargy in support of so critical a part of his President's program as Mutual Security funds. The California Senator's portentous head-shaking over the costs of both foreign aid and national defense at one weekly meeting with the legislators finally exasperated the President to the point of snapping: "My God, you just can't sit back and assume the nation is safe from all harm because the Republicans won the last election!"

The President's own response to such conflicts, however, became somewhat blurred by his own highly personal interpretation of the relationship between the Executive and the Legislature in recent American political history. Quite frequently, he would murmur that Franklin D. Roosevelt had "usurped" powers of the Legislature and that the Congress understandably had felt "deprived" of its "rightful role" for two decades. From this, he inferred a sense of obligation, as President, to redress matters by "restoring" some power to the Legislature. And upon this benevolent vision of Constitutional politics, there intruded no harsh awareness that—from the time of Congress's rebuff to Roosevelt in the historic fight over the Supreme Court—the Executive had never been able, in fact, to move much beyond frontiers guarded by an essentially conservative coalition within the legislature.

The Cabinet provided perhaps the supreme occasion, both practical and symbolic, for the voicing and the enactment of Eisenhower's concept of government. Neither his predecessor nor his successor engaged in any such elaborate exercise: this was peculiar to his approach to the process of governmental decision. It reflected his trust in experts and specialists—a confidence reaffirmed throughout his Administration by every new naming of a special committee, an *ad hoc* commission, or a study group. It translated into political terms his military experience with a staff system, with its promise of work and responsibility lucidly defined, divided, and delegated—so that the commander in chief could confidently expect, from each appropriate aide, either information or action in nicely proportioned spheres of competence. . . .

A historian of a decade hence, however, reviewing . . . all the years of deliberations by Eisenhower Cabinets, would find the narrative punctuated with remarkably few decisions.

Diffuse as were these Cabinet discussions—often as inconclusive as academic seminars—they held a crucial place in Eisenhower's scheme for governing. They fixed the occasions for exchange of facts and views between a President and department heads who, in the majority, had little other opportunity to see and to hear him. Again and again, the President would seize on some particular matter of legislation or administration as spark for a warm homily on his most personal views—the world need for freer trade, or the practical necessity (and "cheapness") of programs of mutual security, or the need to temper austere "businesslike" administration with signs of serious concern for "the little fellow," or the "unthinkable" dimensions of nuclear warfare. For almost all the persons present, these fervent sermons carried an authority almost scriptural. And they tempered, if they did not alter, some of the Cabinet's own generally more conventional predispositions.

Moreover, while these presidential interpolations often might seem to border on the banal, they took on added force because of the repeatedly proven range and specificity of the President's knowledge of the matters confronting the various departments. Practically and detailedly, he would comment on technical procurement problems in Defense or aberrations of the parity laws in Agriculture, the economic impact on New York Harbor of the projected St. Lawrence Seaway or the economic plight of Massachusetts' textile industry, the collapse of zinc prices or the worthlessness of Bolivian tin—and on from there to the warmth of his friendship for Harold Macmillan or his tolerance of the idiosyncracies of Charles De Gaulle.

And the Cabinet served, too, as an arena for conflict, however muted, with the issue of domestic economy vs. world responsibility threatening to trouble the surface of every session. Few men present felt greater distress than Henry Cabot Lodge at the threat of deep cutbacks in expenditures vital to supporting foreign policy. As he heatedly exclaimed to me on one of his weekly visits from the United Nations to the White House: "We are just too damn worried about Taft and the leaders. They don't carry as much weight as they dream—even in the Senate—and they don't matter a *damn* in the country. We won the election despite them, and we can go on winning. Besides, they have *nowhere* to go but to be with *us*. And the one thing we can *not* afford to do is to hand Symington and the Democrats a nice major issue like the charge the 'big business' ideas are shortchanging the nation's security." It was pithily said. But such sentiments seemed smothered in the kind of reviews of the budget that Humphrey impressed upon the Cabinet.

. . . one of the supreme objectives of the Eisenhower presidency . . . was the invigoration and the rejuvenation of the Republican party.

This purpose ended in defeat.

The size of the defeat was easy to measure. The loss of Executive power in the 1960 elections, despite all advantages enjoyed by the incumbent Administration, could not be ascribed, harshly or entirely, to popular distaste for the personality of Richard Nixon. For the signs of Republican weakness and ineptitude were visible almost everywhere across the political landscape. The Republican party that in 1930 claimed governorships in thirty states could boast of merely sixteen in 1960. Of the nation's forty-one major urban centers, the Democrats in 1960 swept a total of twenty-seven. Through all the Eisenhower Years, in fact, the total polling strength of the GOP had steadily declined despite the President's personal electoral triumphs—from 49 percent in 1950, to 47 percent in 1954, finally to 43 percent in 1958. In the Congress convening as Eisenhower left the presidency, the GOP was outnumbered three to two in the House of Representatives and two to one in the Senate. Such a stark reckoning more than sufficed, in short, to justify Eisenhower's own unhappy query to Sherman Adams: "What happened . . . ?"

The answer clearly lay, in great part, with the man who asked the question. The very definition he imposed upon his roles as President and party leader approached a political philosophy of self-denial. Months after leaving office, for example, he was asked if he had "ever sort of turned the screw on Congress to get something done . . . saying you'll withhold an appointment or something like that." And with disarming accuracy, Eisenhower answered: "No, never. I took very seriously the matter of appointments [and] their qualifications. . . . Possibly I was not as shrewd and as clever in this matter as some of the others, but I never thought that any of these appointments should be used for bringing pressure upon the Congress." The President proudly forswearing the use of "pressure," of course, comes close to brusquely renouncing power itself. And such smothering of his own voice must have two inescapable consequences: the floundering of his legislative program in the halls of Congress, and the blurring of his party's image in the eyes of the electorate.

As he treated the political present, so, too Eisenhower faced the future: he served as a passive witness, rather than an aggressive judge, in the choice of leadership to follow him. It is reasonable to accept the sincerity of his belief—by 1960—that "experience" significantly qualified Richard Nixon for the presidency. It is no less certain, however, that—before 1960—Eisenhower constantly reviewed and privately discussed many alternatives to a successor whom he regarded as less than ideal. Along with such personal favorites as Robert Anderson or Alfred Gruenther, he faced . . . the far more serious political possibility of a Nelson Rockefeller. Even if all calculations of simple political success were disregarded . . . the striking fact is that Eisenhower did nothing to encourage his party to weigh such alternatives, even while he pondered them within himself.

The conclusion must be that—for the Republican party under the leadership of Eisenhower—the 1950's essentially were a lost decade. Let the measure be the growth of the party in popular vote or public confidence. Let it be the record of specific legislative achievements. Let it be the less specific but more meaningful matter of clear commitment to abiding principles or exhilarating purposes, relevant to an age of revolution. By all criteria, the judgment must be the same.

And yet, there can be no just criticism of a political leader, obviously, without full reference to the political circumstances. And of the Republican party itself, the serious question must be asked: would some other kind of presidential leadership, more vigorous and more creative, have clearly prevailed over this party's capacity to resist change? The chance of revitalizing a major political organization depends critically upon the nature of the material with which the work must begin. As in this instance, the circumstances confronting Eisenhower might at least be called mitigating.

For the full half-century since the historic struggle of 1912 between Theodore Roosevelt and William Howard Taft, the Republican party has been known to the nation, of course, as the citadel of conservative orthodoxy. In this span of time, it summoned from its own ranks no President who could lay serious historic claim to greatness. It collectively offered no leadership that could be hailed, by a grateful nation, as imaginative, bold, or memorable. For thirty of those years, the party could not win a presidential election except under the leadership of a war hero. Over this same thirty-year period, it held control of the Congress for a meager total of four years. . . .

Yet behind this near-barren half-century, there lies a Republican tradition of a vastly different fiber. This was, almost instantly upon birth, the party that abolished slavery. Throughout the decades of frenetically expanding capitalism . . . this was the party that conceived and wrote the national laws most vital to the public good . . . the first laws of civil service, the anti-trust legislation, the control of the railways, the first federal regulation of food and drugs, the first acts to conserve the nation's natural resources. And throughout this full and rich earlier life the Republican party logically was both the home and the hope ... of the American intellectual.

The third half-century of the story of the Republican party has now just begun. The party, quite obviously, still does not know which of its two selves to *be* in the years immediately ahead. And Dwight David Eisenhower—by his own austere and negative prescription for the role of party leader—could not help it to make up its deeply divided mind. ...

Chapter 14 THE HERO AS POLITICAL LEADER

*Now a columnist and free lance writer, GARRY
WILLS (1934—   ) earned a Ph.D. at Yale
University, taught Classics at The Johns Hopkins
University, and is the author of several books,
including a biography of G. K. Chesterton (1961),*
Politics and Catholic Freedom *(1964),* Roman
Culture *(1966),* Jack Ruby *(1968) and* The Second
Civil War *(1968). In* Nixon Agonistes *(1970) he
analyzed Richard Nixon and contemporary America,
but focuses briefly and incisively on Dwight D.
Eisenhower as a far better politician than Americans
realized. How could a professional soldier acquire
attributes of "political genius"?*

. . . . Eisenhower came up in as rough a school as Lincoln's. He rose in the peacetime professional army, where ambition is thwarted of its natural object (excellence
in war) and falls back on jealousy and intrigue. Eisenhower climbed that slippery
ladder of bayonets with a sure step and rare instinct for survival. His basic shrewdness came out in many ways. In his great success at poker and bridgee for instance.
Like Nixon, he made large sums of money in the long games at military bases.
Unlike Nixon, he was so good he had to stop playing with enlisted men; he was
leaving too many of them broke.

The survival instinct shows, also, in his concern for being properly armed at all
times. In his autobiography, he claims that he learned this lesson as a child in a
barnyard: a goose used to attack and torment him, until he learned that a broom in
his hand would make the bird keep its distance. From that time he never went out

the door without a broom in his fist: "I quickly learned never to negotiate with an adversary except from a position of strength." Years later he recalled, quite casually, that as President of Columbia he did not venture onto the streets of New York at night without his service revolver in his pocket. His life in the interval had been studiously devoted to keeping the right broom in his hand at all times.

He was master of the essentials. The most successful warrior in the modern world, he never romanticized war. His head was not dizzied with MacArthur's visions of glory. There were no screaming trumpets in his rhetoric. He preferred drums; and even his interest in those did not date from West Point parades, but from high school days in Kansas. "They used a drum to rally us in ranks for reentering the school after a play time. The drummer could turn the tumult of a recess crowd into some semblance of quiet, orderly movement. I've always admired the drum since and despised the siren. The drum communicates a message and calms as it warns. In later years, when well-intentioned escorts elected to use a siren on my behalf, I asked—or ordered—that it be stopped."

As an athlete, he was efficient rather than spectacular: "I was good at bat, trained by my coach as a 'chop hitter'—to poke the ball, in effect, at selected spots in the field, rather than swinging freely away." Speaking of the rigors of plebe year at the Point, he writes: "I suppose that if any time had been provided to sit down and think for a moment, most of the 285 of us would have taken the next train out. But no one was given much time to think—and when I did it was always, 'Where else could you get a college education without cost?' " No love affair with the uniform or his trade's glamour. Asked at the end of his course to list the three assignments he most aspired to, in order of preference, he put down "*Infantry* first, *Infantry* second, and *Infantry* third." He volunteered for cook's school, and first distinguished himself as a supply officer. The second thing he became known for in the army was a series of assignments to coach football teams.

His third, and major, speciality may surprise those who think of him as tongue-tied and vague. The disjointed syntax of Eisenhower's press conferences and aphasia after his stroke in 1957 helped to create the picture of Eisenhower as a benevolent but rather goofy, grandfatherly type. Yet his principal army work, before the war, was, as a writer. Not much for books during his days at West Point, he became a student of military history afterward, while stationed in Panama. This led him to General Staff School at Fort Leavenworth in 1925. Though he had been low in his class at the Point, he ranked high in this "graduate school" of ambitious young officers seeking promotion. The commandant of the school wanted him to stay on as an instructor. Instead, he was sent to France, to write a guidebook on American action there during World War I. That is how he came to know the continent he would later invade. Then his writing duties were extended to the drafting of speeches and letters—and even of two chapters of autobiography—for

General Pershing. After that, he served briefly with the Assistant Secretary of War, before Douglas MacArthur asked for his services as a writer of letters and memoranda.

Eisenhower opposed MacArthur's plan to make a personal appearance in the rebuff of Coxey's [sic] Army from Washington; but despite this difference, and a general clash of temperaments, MacArthur requested Ike's further services when he went to the Philippines. While he was there, Eisenhower learned to fly and logged 350 hours as a pilot. Even after World War II, he used to go up and take over the controls of planes—until the advent of jets. He had always been an excellent horseman; and earlier, he and George Patton had pioneered, on their own, some experiments in the maneuver and servicing of tanks. Eisenhower also helped direct the first transcontinental convoy of army trucks. He found time, somewhere along the line, to learn at first hand the use of all his professional tools—from the galley stove to airplane carburetors.

Looking back on his days in the Philippines, Eisenhower told Arthur Larson: "You know that General MacArthur got quite a reputation as a silver-tongued speaker when he was in the Philippines. Who do you think wrote his speeches? I did." Both Larson and Emmet Hughes spent hours with Eisenhower, working over successive drafts of the presidential speeches; and they both, despite very different political estimates of the man, agree that he had rare discrimination in the use of the written word. He hated imprecision and was a stickler for grammatical niceties. He disliked gaudy and inflated phrases, and had a disconcerting way of asking political speech writers, who tend to get carried away by their own rhetoric, what a high-sounding phrase might *mean*. When Hughes opened a speech with "The world and we have passed the mid-century point of a century of continuing challenge," Eisenhower penned in a margin: "I hate this sentence. *Who* challenges *whom*? *What about*?" Emmet Hughes is a professional journalist, used to the ministrations—blunt or subtle—of professional editors. It is interesting, then, that he found Eisenhower a particularly good editor. . . .

What, then, is one to make of those famous meanderings at press conferences? They were a proof of Eisenhower's sense of priorities. He was intensely briefed by twenty or thirty staff experts before each press conference. He went into each session with certain things clearly in mind—things he was determined to say, and the way they should be said; things he was determined not to say, and ways to circle around them. And he got the job done. The rest was fluff and filler—but fluff under control. Even Hughes, Eisenhower's critic, grants that he "made not one politically significant verbal blunder throughout eight years of press conferences and public addresses." And Larson points out that the troublesome phrases of the Eisenhower regime were not blurted by the President, as in Truman's time; they were coined by the scholarly Secretary of State, who put "the brink" and "massive retaliation" and "agonizing reappraisal" in circulation.

Eisenhower revealed his conscious strategy in these matters during the tense days of the Quemoy-Matsu crisis. His press secretary, James Hagerty, advised him to take a no-comment stand on the whole issue. " 'Don't worry, Jim,' I told him as we went out the door. 'If that question comes up, I'll just confuse them.' " An example of this calculated obfuscation occurred in the 1952 race. Eisenhower, not much liking the task, was set to campaign with Senator William Jenner, who had called Ike's old friend and boss, General Marshall, a traitor. Journalist Murray Kempton, trying to put Eisenhower on the spot, asked the candidate at a press conference in Denver what he thought of men who call Marshall a traitor. Eisenhower engaged in a rare bit of public scenery-chewing: no one should even *mention* such false charges. He seemed almost to swoon with pious detestation—yet he was careful not to mention Jenner. All the onus of slander was shifted to the journalist for raising such a question. After the conference, Ike grinned and shook hands with Kempton, making him realize what a skilled performance this was.

Eisenhower's relations with Nixon cannot be estimated until we realize that his remarks, his silences were, on key matters, conscious and chosen things.

The one thing Eisenhower regularly entrusted to Nixon was housekeeping work in the Republican Party. The Vice-President was given the thankless task of campaigning for every Republican in America on off-years, when the ticket, without Eisenhower's magic name at the top, took woeful beatings. If Eisenhower needed Right-Wing support, Nixon was dispatched to round it up. That was true at the time of the Korean peace settlement, which Senator Knowland attacked as a "peace without honor." It was true in debates over the Bricker Amendment and foreign aid. It was especially true when the White House had to deal with Joseph McCarthy.

Nixon realized these were dirty missions he was sent on, but necessary ones. His complaint was that Eisenhower did not seem to grasp their crucial nature, or value the man who could accomplish them. That is why he continued to think Eisenhower a professional soldier and an amateur politician. But Eisenhower was almost the opposite of "a plain blunt soldier." What he grasped was that partisan loyalty, the essential source of reward or punishment at lower levels, can be an encumbrance at the very top—useful at times, of course, but also dangerous. He retained loyalty through the action of subordinates; but protected himself from any danger by keeping those subordinates at arm's length, always ready to sacrifice them. He was just as willing to drop Sherman Adams, or undercut the proud rhetoric of Foster Dulles, as he had been to dump Nixon in 1952 and 1956.

A difference in attitude toward "politics" is only one aspect of the barrier that existed between Eisenhower and Nixon, preventing mutual understanding (for Eisenhower as surely underestimated Nixon as Nixon did his boss). The Vice-President of the fifties was a "hard worker," not merely in the obvious sense that he worked hard; he wanted the work to show; he needed to convince people of his earnestness and effort. This not only impressed others, it convinced *him* that he had earned what he aimed for.

Though he was not given to boasting or superlatives—Larson says he cut anything out of speech drafts that sounded like "I always" or "I never"—Eisenhower nonetheless told Emmet Hughes: "The fact remains that he [John Foster Dulles] just knows more about foreign affairs than anybody I know. In fact, I'll be immodest and say that there's only one man I know who has seen more of the world and talked with more people and *knows* more than he does—and that's me." Eisenhower was often represented, during his years in office, as the captive of Dulles in foreign policy. But historical perspective and the appearance of contemporaries' accounts are making it clear that Ike weighed shrewdly the strong and weak points of Dulles. Not only did he take positions opposed to his Secretary of State's; he did it with serene confidence in his own judgment. That was true in such matters as the Korean settlement, the encouragement of cultural exchange with Russia, the treatment of the French over Indochina, and the handling of Khrushchev's visit to America. Murray Kempton, in a brilliant essay called "The Underestimation of Dwight D. Eisenhower" (*Esquire*, September 1967), puts it well: "Never thereafter could he contemplate the war in Indochina except in the frozen tones of a War College report on a maneuver by officers who can henceforth abandon all hope of promotion. The French, he instructs Foster Dulles, have committed the classic military blunder. In Geneva, Dulles is said to have hinted that the United States might use the atom bomb to save the French; there is no evidence that he would have dared transmit that suggestion to a President who plainly would not have trusted him with a stick of dynamite to blow up a fish pond."

One of the results of Eisenhower's derided staff system was that he knew how to deal with experts, to evaluate competing ones, and not to be intimidated by them. His brother, Edgar Eisenhower, tried to pull rank on the Bricker Amendment, arguing that he knew more about the law because he was a lawyer. Ike answered that this matter transcended legal niceties and moved up into the area where he, Ike, was the expert. The staff system was not a way of avoiding action, as many charged (though it allowed him to evade responsibility in the sense that, if any head had to roll, it would not be his). Emmet Hughes poses the standard argument against Eisenhower—one which resembles, in some ways, the opinion of Hughes' political enemy, Nixon. After noting that Eisenhower had more power and popularity than any recent President, he says: "Yet it had been the pattern of action, if not the purpose of the man, to husband and to guard these resources—like savings earned by the sweat of a lifetime—so that they not be spent in the rough and contaminating play of power and politics." Hughes fails to appreciate that the conservation of authority—or, rather, the reconstitution of it—deserved the high priority Eisenhower gave it. He took over a nation full of internal doubt and suspicion, summarized (often melodramatically) in the phrase "the McCarthy Era."

So successfully did Ike quiet this divisive ferment that his critics would, by the end of his time in office, reproach him for running such a quiet ship. It was a substantial achievement, though not a flashy one. In his customary manner, Ike got the job done, without trumpets. In his foreign policy, he inherited the Cold War and brought a degree of stability and—once again—placidity to the handling of conflicts. He took over a nation at war, a people fearful of atomic holocaust and poisoned milk. He left office to a man who cried for more missiles and for shock troops to fight guerrilla wars by helicopter.

Arthur Larson devotes a whole chapter of his book *Eisenhower: The President Nobody Knew* to a refutation of the Hughes argument against "conserving power." He contrasts Ike's handling of the Lebanon crisis with Kennedy's Bay of Pigs fiasco and Johnson's intervention in the Dominican Republic. And he contrasts the Eisenhower attitude toward Indochina with his successor's willingness to get involved in Vietnam. In Lebanon Eisenhower combined limited aim, conciliatory rhetoric, and appeals to the UN, with massive sudden troop presence—walking far more softly than Teddy Roosevelt did, but carrying a big stick. His attitude toward the crisis was summed up in *Waging Peace*:

> The basic mission of United States forces in Lebanon was not primarily to fight. Every effort was made to have our landing be as much of a garrison move as possible. In my address I had been careful to use the term "stationed" in Lebanon . . . If it had been prudent, I would have preferred that the first battalion ashore disembark at a dock rather than across the beaches. However, the attitude of the Lebanese army was at that moment unknown, and it was obviously wise to disembark in deployed formation ready for any emergency. As it turned out, there was no resistance; the Lebanese along the beaches welcomed our troops. The geographic objectives of the landing included only the city of Beirut and the adjoining airfield . . . The decision to occupy only the airfield and capital was a political one which I adhered to over the recommendations of the military. If the Lebanese army were unable to subdue the rebels when we had secured their capital and protected their government, I felt, we were backing up a government with so little popular support that we probably should not be there.

Once, when Eisenhower was complaining about the "tyranny" of weak nations who can pester giants with impunity, he ended his tirade with the calm shrug: "We must put up with it." There is a world of neglected wisdom in that statement. It underlies Eisenhower's warnings against a land war in Asia, his refusal to fight wars in which the enemy has choice of weapons and terrain and times. When Eisenhower moved, he made sure he had the broom in his hand—army, navy, air force, and marines to Lebanon (over 14,000 men) with back-up troops assembling—or he did not move at all. He was not tortured by the fear of "losing face." His attitude toward the cover story for Francis Gary Powers was typical of him. ("Cut your losses" is the motto Kempton finds for many of his actions). He had only one criticism of the Army in its fight with McCarthy: on the disastrous promotion of Peress, he advised the Army "to admit its mistake and then stand its ground." By trying to cover up the bungling, Secretary Stevens just got further entangled.

The common note in all these matters is Eisenhower's resolute lack of romanticism (it is no accident that he changed Roosevelt's name—Shangri-La—for the presidential retreat in Maryland). Contrast this realism with the sweeping pronouncements of his successors, who dealt in overkill rhetoric (Kennedy's inaugural "this hemisphere intends to remain the master of its own house") They walked noisily and carried little sticks. Lyndon Johnson's "We will always oppose the effort of one nation to conquer another" puts us forever at the mercy of tyrannical weak nations.

Headier stuff, this, than the yawning years of Eisenhower. But Eisenhower must have heard the rhetoric of endless young officers, would-be MacArthurs who dashed into their own Bays of Pigs, when Kennedy orated that "Now the trumpet summons us again." Kennedy seemed almost to long for adversity: "In the long history of the world, only a few generations have been granted the role of defending freedom in its hour of maximum danger. I do not shrink from this responsibility [another hit at the supposedly do-nothing Ike]; I welcome it." One suspects that the old man on the platform felt bemused and rather sorry for the new President who literally did not know what he was asking for. One of Kennedy's first acts when he came into office was to "free" the government from reliance on massive response to military threat; he equipped the nation to go by helicopter into jungles with the assault force Generals Gavin and Taylor had recommended much to Eisenhower's horror as a professional soldier. . . .

Chapter 15 EISENHOWER EXPLAINS HIS OWN ROLE

DWIGHT D. EISENHOWER *(1890-1969), 34th President of the United States, graduated from West Point in 1915 and spent most of his adult life as a career army officer. He directed the invasions of North Africa, Italy and France during World War II and served as chief of staff of the U. S. Army, 1945-1948. He became president of Columbia University in 1948 but returned to active duty in 1950 as commander of NATO forces in Europe, resigning from the army to run for the presidency in 1952. Much of his army career at higher levels dealt with political matters, including relations with wartime allies and military reorganization and funding after 1945. Though critics accused Eisenhower of uttering unintelligible prose, he did explain his views in news conferences held almost every week of his presidency; excerpts from these press conferences form the next selection. How did Eisenhower define his own role as a political leader? Do his words confirm or refute Garry Wills' analysis of the previous selection?*

March 5, 1953:

The President: I have always supported and insisted upon the right of the Congress to conduct such investigations as it sees fit. I think it is inherent in its powers and its responsibilities. Now, when it gets into fields in which I think some misunderstanding or damage or difficulty can arise, why, I have to watch it—do my best to show them my convictions. But I don't believe it is really a proper thing for me to be discussing publicly a coordinate branch of Government. If ever I find that necessary, it will be through some change of views. I try to avoid it.

Public Papers of the Presidents of the United States: Dwight D. Eisenhower (Washington, 1958-1961), *1953*, pp. 88, 474; *1954*, pp. 50-51; 545-546; *1956*, p. 891; *1957*, pp. 353, 399-401, 576-577; *1958*, pp. 265-266, 828-832; *1959*, pp. 366-367, 537-538, 545, 574-575; *1960*, p. 680.

July 8, 1953

The President: I don't consider it my function to interfere in the local and State elections. After all, there are certain responsibilities placed upon the President of the United States. There are certain attitudes I think that he is expected normally to observe. I hope to do that.

Now, my own contention is this: the only worthwhile political program, particularly for the party in power, is to present at each new election, to the people of the United States, an accomplishment, a worthwhile progress that earns approbation. I can see no other way of approaching the thing, and I don't see how the President could interfere or attempt to interfere appropriately in the local political struggles —city, county, State, or anything of that kind.

January 13, 1954:

The President. . . . within reason, I think we know and can identify those features of bills or of a legislative program that could be classed as "must." They are the things that have to be done. Now, there are certain things which I believe are for the good of the country. I have arrived at those conclusions after long study with all my associates, . . . and I am going to fight for them where I think they are important. I naturally cannot tell you in advance which I am going to consider the most important and the least important. I don't know how they will come up in Congress and how they will be handled. So I am not going to identify particular details as "must" and "not must" except as they apply to supply bills, legislative bills, security bills in their main outline, such things as that, or where laws expire and something has to be done. . . .

June 10, 1954:

Q. . . . in 1953 you said during the course of the campaign that you endorsed all Republican candidates for the House and Senate. . . . I just wondered if you feel that same way this year?

The President: Well, you are asking me a question that I dislike just answering in great generality. I did say that I endorsed the candidates nominated by the Republicans of their districts and States . . . because of my earnest belief that the legislative body should be controlled through its committees and organization by the same party that provides the occupant of the White House; that if that were not true, there was always an opportunity to dodge party responsibility. Of course, in that sense, I still believe the same thing, that the Republicans as long as they are in power ought to be in power and be held responsible for every action or lack of action that you can trace to them.

October, 11, 1956:

Q. Do you agree that McCarthy and Jenner and Malone fit in with your picture of the new Republican party?

The President: Let's remember, there are no national parties in the United States.

There are 48 State parties, and they are the ones that determine the people that belong to those parties.

There is nothing I can do to say that one is not a Republican. The most I can say is that in many things they do not agree with me. Therefore, in looking for help to get over a program, which is the sole purpose of political leadership, as I see it, for the good of the country, I can't look to them for help.

May 15, 1957:

Q. The roll call votes in Congress so far this year show that the Democrats are supporting your program more than the Republicans. Do you intend now or as the '58 elections approach to punish those Republicans who are not supporting your program or to reward those who do support you?

The President: I don't think it is the function of a President of the United States to punish anybody for voting what he believes.

Q. Sir, Republican Senators Clifford Case, Cooper, Javits, Bush and some others have steadfastly supported your program, most particularly the budget, and in doing so they put themselves at odds with the Senate Republican leadership. I wonder, sir, if you have any particular plans or new plans to work with them or through them to gain enactment of your program.

The President: I don't see how it is possible for any President to work with the Republican group in Congress, the whole Republican group, except through their elected leadership. Now, this doesn't mean that in special cases and for special purposes you don't, but always with the knowledge of the leadership, see people and try to influence them in your direction.

May 22, 1957:

Q. Leaving out the question . . . of punishment, would you be more disposed to support those who do back your program and less disposed to back those who do not, next year?

The President: Well, if you want to make that statement within reasonable—and what I would call logical—grounds, I think it will be a pity if ever we tried to organize in this country political parties that are based upon slavish adherence to every detail and concept of government that can be advanced, because then you will have nothing but a whole group of splinter parties. . . . Therefore, each party should encompass a very great deal—I mean a very wide range—of political thinking. But, I do believe this: when a political party gets together and agrees upon a platform and that platform is presented to the American public as the political basis on which they are going to try to conduct the Government if elected, they should remain true to it. I believe they should stick with it . . . unless conditions so change that anyone would understand that some change would have to be made. . . .

So, I have no right and no desire to punish anybody. I just say this: I am committed to the support of the people who believe, as I do, that the Republican platform of 1956 must be our political doctrine.

Q. . . . . in that connection, it has been suggested . . . that Senator Knowland should resign as majority leader because he is opposed to so much of your program. Would you care to comment on that?

The President: The organization of the Senate and of the political parties within the Senate is a matter for Senate decision and for the party decision in the Senate. It has never even crossed my mind to ask the resignation of anybody because they are not direct subordinates of mine.

Now, I do believe this: that if you will look up the record you will find that, at least Senator Knowland not long ago said this, that his record of support for things which I have advocated was very good indeed, the highest percentage, I believe he said, in the Senate.

He has differed with me on some very important points, and I think some of them are critical and they represent real differences, but it does not mean that he is my enemy. It means that he has got some very strong convictions on the other side of the fence.

Q. . . . in previous elections . . . you have always supported every Republican who was running for the Senate or the House without regard to their voting record. I am wondering whether that will continue to be your attitude in '58. . . .

The President: Now, I hope that I will never be accused of being so namby-pamby that I don't have degrees of enthusiasm about people that stand with me and those that stand against me.

Now, what I do want to make clear is this: I most earnestly believe that the Congress and the White House should be occupied and controlled by the same party, whenever this is humanly possible that this could be done, for the reason then you can fix responsiblity.

July 31, 1957:

Q. . . . just before the House killed that school bill, the Democrats came around to the support of the Administration's bill. They are willing to go along with your bill; and their complaint is that you failed to go to bat for the legislation. . . .

The President: I spoke up plenty of times for the principles in which I believe. But, I say, I realize I can't get exactly what I want, so I have compromised twice in the proposals that I have placed before the Congress, and I was even ready to accept even further proposals. But I am getting to the point where I can't be too enthusiastic about something that I think is likely to fasten a sort of an albatross . . . around the neck of the Federal Government. . . . And I tell you this: I will have another bill ready for the next session of Congress.

Q. The friends of the school bill say that you failed to use your influence, and if you had, you could have gotten the bill you wanted. . . . On the other hand, in the Senate yesterday, Senator Russell complained because he said you were using your influence for the civil rights. Could you compare where you do and when you don't use your influence?

The President: Well, ... with respect to the school bill, it is true I put it in two or three State of the Union speeches. I went before the public on a television speech about the budget and put this item before the public again. I went over to the Statler Hotel and addressed a large educational meeting on the same thing. I never wavered in exactly what I am trying to do.

Mostly the work of a President with Congress in my opinion is done in a quiet conversational way by the telephone and informal meetings. You don't influence Congress, in my opinion, by threats, by anything except trying to convince them of the soundness and the logic of your views.

Now, in one case here, I have done it. In the other case, I have done it; but in one case apparently your words are more publicized and people get an idea you are more for this than that. I don't make distinctions of that kind. I am trying to get through a program that I have constantly put before the Congress and I believe to be for the good of the United States, and I will talk to any Congressman that is on the Hill about these things if he has got any honest differences of conviction with me. I try to do it, and I try to win their votes over, but I don't get up and make statements every twenty minutes.

April 2, 1958:

Q. ... Senator Styles Bridges was asked if he thought there was a "palace guard," and he said he thought there might be at times information withheld from you purposely by some members of this "palace guard." ... and I wondered if you take precautions to see that you get information, not just from one or two channels, but from a variety of sources.

The President: You know, sometimes it seems almost useless to try to answer questions because the answer to me seems so obvious. Now, since 1941 I have been in a position where I have had to use staffs; and certainly if I were not kept well acquainted with the basic facts of my problem, then I would have certainly been ineffective, and at least on a few occasions I think we did a little bit better than average.

Now, this business of "palace guard" is like other expressions that we get in the habit of using ... that to my mind have no meaning. Of course you have to have a staff. And it would be ridiculous to think that everything that each member of that staff heard had to be repeated to me each day in that office. I would never have anybody else in there, because they hear everything.

Now, they do sort out the things that are interesting to Government and to me and make certain that I get them, whether they are recommendations from important people or ideas or facts or statistics, anything else.

But on top of the "palace guard," that you want to call it—I have the National Security Council, I have the Cabinet, and on top of that I have this: direct orders to every member of an executive department or independent agency that he can come to me directly at any time and no staff officer can stand in his way.

November 5, 1958:

Q. . . . do you think that the people yesterday chose left-wing government rather than sensible government?

The President: I think at least this: I don't know whether they did this thing deliberately. I know this, that they obviously voted for people that I would class among the spenders, and that is what I say is going to be the real trouble. And I promise this: for the next 2 years, the Lord sparing me, I am going to fight this as hard as I know how.

Q. Sir, after some of your campaigning, do you anticipate additional trouble with the Democratic Congress this time?

The President: Not at all. I have always dealt with the Democratic Congress in what I thought, in my honest conviction, was good for the country, and I think there are a lot of them believe that they want to do what is good for the country. I assure you again that I'm talking about a good many people in that party.

Q. . . . what do you think was the primary reason that so many Democrats were elected? Was it local issues or was it perhaps disenchantment with the administration nationally?

The President: Well, so far as I know, I have never varied in my basic convictions as to the functions of the Federal Government in our country and in my beliefs as to what is the great, broad, middle-of-the-road that the United States should be following.

I have preached this as loudly as I could for 6 years. Now, after 4 years of that kind of teaching, the United States did give me, after all, a majority of I think well over nine million votes.

Here, only 2 years later, there is a complete reversal; and yet I do not see where there is anything that these people consciously want the administration to do differently. And, if I am wrong, I'd like to know what it is; but I am trying to keep the fiscal soundness in this country and to try to keep the economy on a good level keel and to work for peace. Now, if they want me to do anything else, I don't know exactly what it is.

July 22, 1959:

Q. Could you give us some of your thinking on the use of the veto as an administrative device? Do you agree with Woodrow Wilson that it is perhaps the strongest weapon in the hands of a President. . . . and how bad does a bill have to be before you'll resort to a veto?

The President: You're asking a question in a generality that can't be answered accurately except in specifics. The bill has to be in front of you. What does it do to the United States? What does it purport to do for a particular group, or what else does it do?

I have said time and time again that it is clear that I am, or the Presidency is, a part of the legislative process, so stated by the Constitution; it states just exactly how he may act and then what Congress can do.

And if he didn't exercise his own judgment as to what is best for his country in this case, I think he'd be derelict of his duty. . . .

August 12, 1959:

Q. In recent weeks, sir . . . many of us have been invited to . . . the White House, and to speak with you personally . . . and also you have now instituted . . . a new form of diplomacy by travel around the world. You have set a very heavy schedule for yourself. And you are participating with great vigor in domestic affairs.

And I was wondering, sir, if you could explain to us whether this apparent new departure for you is due perhaps to a new concept in your own mind of the Presidency. . . .

The President: Well, I think it is perfectly simple. I have told you people several times that I believe the Presidency should be relieved of detail and many of its activities by proper officials who can take delegated authority and exercise it in his name. But when you have a situation that has gone on, as we have had this cold war since 1945 . . . it becomes the kind of a stalemate that . . . has the element of almost hopelessness for people, and finally becomes something there must be no gun unfired and no individual effort spared in order to break that kind of a stalemate. So the only thing here is that I am trying to end the stalemate and to bring people together more ready to talk.

Now when you talk about the domestic field, the situation is somewhat different. But let us remember that if I live to finish my tour, there will only be 25 per cent of that tour in which I have had a Congress of the same political party as myself. Therefore, it becomes more and more difficult, I think, as time goes on, to get understandings and to get progress in legislation that will be helpful for the country. And I think it takes, therefore, possibly more personal activity than I think would be normal in more normal circumstances.

September 7, 1960:

Q. Sir, it's often been said that you preferred to stand above politics. I wonder if you would give us your views on the role of the Presidency in political campaigns, and would you tell us whether you personally enjoy political activities?

The President: Well, first of all, I of course am not responsible for the opinions of others saying I like to stay above politics. I've never said so. I recognize that I have, or have had the responsibility to be the head of the party, a party that upholds the basic philosophy that I believe to be correct for application in this Nation. . . .

Now, believing that, and having been responsible for directing the operations of the executive department for the past 7½ years, it would be odd if I simply became a sphinx and refused to show why I believe these things and what were my hopes for it in the future. Now, I do think this: I think that the President, as long as he is President, still has an obligation to every single individual in this Nation. Therefore, the rule of reason and of logic and of good sense has got to apply in these things if a man in such position, concerned with the dignity of the office, concerned with its standing, he cannot just go out and be in the hustings and shouting some of the things that we see stated often irresponsibly. I believe he does have a right to make his views known to Americans wherever they are.

Part Five   THE EISENHOWER-DULLES FOREIGN POLICIES

Chapter 16 THE BASES OF AMERICAN POLICY

Eisenhower's Secretary of State, 1953-1959, JOHN
FOSTER DULLES *(1888-1959) came from a
diplomatic family. His grandfather, John W. Foster,
was Secretary of State under President Benjamin
Harrison and held other diplomatic posts. An uncle,
Robert Lansing, was Secretary of State under
Woodrow Wilson, 1915-1920, and Dulles' brother
Allen became head of the Central Intelligence
Agency. A specialist in international law, Dulles was a
member of the prominent firm of Sullivan and
Cromwell, 1911-1949, accompanied his uncle to the
Paris peace conference in 1919, represented the
United States at the San Francisco conference on the
United Nations in 1945 and in the U. N. general
assembly between 1946 and 1950, and negotiated the
treaty of peace with Japan in 1951. He wrote two
books on international affairs,* War, Peace and Change
(1939) and War or Peace *(1950). In these remarks
Dulles presents his views on the aims of United States
foreign policy, the purpose of American military
strength and the fundamental goals of America itself.
How do these principles fit prevailing American
views, and how did Dulles relate them to international
problems?*

Before the National War College, June, 16, 1953:

I should like to talk for a few minutes about power in a material sense, such as is
represented by our splendid military establishment. What is the purpose of this
power? Admiral Mahan is credited with one of the best answers to this question. It
is that the role of power is to give moral ideas the time to take root. Where moral
ideas already are well-rooted, there is little occasion for much military or police
force. We see that illustrated in our own communities. Where the people accept the
moral law and its great commandments, where they exercise self-control and self-
discipline, then there is very little need for police power. Under these circum-

John Foster Dulles, "Morals and Power," *Department of State Bulletin,* XXVII (June 29,
1953), 895-897; "The Challenge of Change," *Department of State Bulletin,* XXXVIII (June 23,
1958), 1035-1042.

stances, it is sufficient to have a very modest force to take care of the small minority always found in every community which disregards the precepts of the moral law.

Where, however, there are many who do not accept moral principles, then that creates the need of force to protect those who do. That, unfortunately, is the case in the world community of today.

At the present time, there is no moral code which has worldwide acceptance. The principles upon which our society is based ... which we believe to be both humanitarian and just—are not accepted by governments which dominate more than one-third of mankind.

The result is that we have a world which is, for the most part, split between two huge combinations. On the one hand, there is the United States and its free-world associates. This is a voluntary alliance of free peoples working together in the recognition that without unity there could be catastrophe.

On the other hand, there is the totalitarian bloc led by the Soviet Union—an artificial, imposed unity which cannot be called an alliance in the sense that we use the word.

These huge concentrations are in conflict because each reflects differing aims, aspirations, and social, political, and economic philosophies. We must assume that they will continue to remain in basic conflict, in one way or another, until such time as the Communists so change their nature as to admit that those who wish to live by the moral law are free to do so without coercion by those who believe in enforced conformity to a materialistic standard.

The entire creed of Soviet communism is based upon ... "dialectical materialism," the theory that there is no such thing as a moral law or spiritual truth; that all things are predetermined by the contradictory movements of matter; that so-called capitalism is historically fated to collapse; and that communism is the movement predestined to effect that collapse.

Now, let us look briefly at another of the springs of Soviet action, that of historical imperialism. This urge to expand is not something patented by the Communists of Soviet Russia. This urge has long been found with the "Great Russians" in the Eurasian heartland. It is a national urge, though it is clear that today communism has greatly intensified it.

The third and last influence ... is that chronic sense of insecurity which pervades police-state rulers. Those who rule by force invariably fear force. In a police state the rulers have a monopoly or near monopoly of weapons. But it is never possible to arm enough policemen to rule an unruly mass without in the process arming some who themselves may prove unruly. Also, the rulers of a police state greatly fear any weapons which they do not control, and they seek to extend their power to bring these weapons under control. They cannot imagine that armaments in the hands of others may be designed purely for internal security and self-defense. That is why the Soviet leaders have so consistently and so violently expressed their opposition to the North Atlantic Treaty Organization and fought the creation of a European Defense Community. To us their fears seem mere pretense. But perhaps they do have fear, because they do not understand that if force is in the hands of those who are governed by moral law, it will not be used as a means of aggression or to violate the principles of the moral law.

The great weakness of Soviet Communist doctrine is that it denies morality. That is its Achilles heel, of which we must take advantage. We can take advantage of it if—but only if—we ourselves accept the supremacy of moral law.

Our nation was founded by the men who believed that there was a Divine Creator who endowed men with unalienable rights. They believed, as George Washington put it in his farewell address, that religion and morality are the great pillars of human happiness and that morality cannot prevail in exclusion of religious principles.

Our Federal and State Constitutions, our laws and practices, reflect the belief that there is a Being superior to ourselves who has established His own laws which can be comprehended by all human beings and that human practices should seek conformity with those laws.

Seeking first the Kingdom of God and His righteousness, many material things were added to us. We developed here an area of spiritual, intellectual, and material richness, the like of which the world has never seen. What we did caught the imagination of men everywhere and became known everywhere as "the Great American Experiment." Our free society became a menace to every despot because we showed how to meet the hunger of the people for greater opportunity and for greater dignity. The tide of despotism, which at that time ran high, was rolled back and we ourselves enjoyed security.

We need to recapture that mood.

Today some seem to feel that Americanism means being tough and "hard-boiled," doing nothing unless we are quite sure that it is to our immediate short-term advantage; boasting of our own merit and seeing in others only demerit.

That is a caricature of America. Our people have always been generous to help, out of their abundance, those who are the victims of misfortune. Our forebears have traditionally had what the Declaration of Independence refers to as a decent respect for the opinion of mankind. They sought to practice the Golden Rule by doing to others as they would have others do unto them. Their conduct and example made our nation one that was respected and admired through the world.

Before the Senate Foreign Relations Committee, June 6, 1958:

United States foreign policy is designed to protect and promote the interests of the United States in the international field. It is based upon certain facts and convictions:

(a) That the peoples of the world universally desire the elimination of war and the establishment of a just peace;

(b) That the designs of aggressive Communist imperialism pose a continuous threat to every nation of the free world, including our own;

(c) That the security of this nation can be maintained only by the spiritual, economic, and military strength of the free world, with this nation a powerful partner committed to this purpose;

(d) That change is a law of life, for nations as well as for men, and that no political, economic, or social system survives unless it proves its continuing worth in the face of ever-changing circumstances;

(e) That the effectiveness of our collective-security measures depends upon the economic advancement of the less developed parts of the free world, which strengthens their purpose and ability to sustain their independence;

(f) That in all international associations and combinations within the free world, of which the United States is a member, it considers all nations, including itself, as equals. The sovereignty of no nation will ever be limited or diminished by any act of the United States.

The interests of the United States, which our foreign policy would safeguard and promote, include:

The lives and homes of our people; their confidence and peace of mind; their economic well-being; and their ideals.

These interests are not mutually exclusive; rather they are overlapping and interdependent. Yet, of them, ideals rank first.

Our people have never hesitated to sacrifice life, property, and economic well-being in order that our ideals should not perish from the earth.

So we often have a narrow path to tread. We must avoid war and still stand firm and affirmative for what we deem to be just and right.

We face the challenge of change. Long-established political relationships are evaporating; massive, fresh human aspirations demand new responses; physical limitations within and without this globe are being swept away by the advances of science.

1. We are witnessing a political revolution that is drastic and worldwide in its repercussions. For 500 years Europe was predominant in the world through a political system known as colonialism, backed by preponderant industrial and military power.

That political system is now in process of rapid transformation. Within the last 15 years 700 million people of 20 countries have won political independence. This trend will continue.

But stability is not achieved and a new order comfortably established merely by the grant of political independence. This is but the beginning of a two-phased struggle.

To preserve political independence requires a people who themselves exercise self-restraint and who acquire education. without these qualities, political independence may mean but a brief transition from benevolent colonialism to ruthless dictatorship.

The second front is the economic front. The grant of independence has generated mass aspirations, which spread contagiously to all who, having been bogged down for centuries in a morass of abject poverty, demand a prospect for rising in the economic scale.

2. We face another new world in terms of physical power. The splitting of the atom revealed sources of power so vast, so omnipresent, as to imply a new industrial revolution. Also it changes the very nature of war, in that general war now menaces the very existence of human life upon this planet.

3. A third new world opens in terms of outer space. . . . Just what this means we do not know. We sense but dimly what we realize must be new possibilities of infinite purport.

4. Even on this globe, old areas take on new aspects. What were barriers of forbidding cold and ice snow, in the north, offer the routes whereby many can most quickly establish contact with each other. And in the south, Antarctica, probed by the Geophysical Year, reveals a new and exciting possibility of service to mankind.

5. And peace must be better assured within the society of nations.

Today no international wars are being fought. For that we can be thankful. But our peace is a precarious peace, because it rests too much on individual and national restraints, upon accurate calculations, and upon avoidance of miscalculations and mischances. It is not sufficiently rooted in a system of law, order, and justice.

The United States responds to the challenge of change. As an equal among equals, and in willing partnership with others, we play a positive and creative part. We do so not merely as a counter to Communist imperialism. We do so because to play such a part is natural to us. . . .

We realize full well that the solid establishment of independence is a hard task. We take every appropriate occasion to assist it.

We encourage educational exchanges and "leader" visits.

We provide technical assistance, both bilaterally and through the United Nations.

We provide funds for economic development. Private capital plays the primary role, but the Export-Import Bank and the Development Loan Fund are essential supplements.

The leaders of the new countries are not blind to the danger to independence that stems from international communism. They seek to find, in freedom, the way to solve their countries' problems. They look to the United States as the nation from which they can most dependably obtain assistance which will add to, not subtract from, their lasting independence.

The United States pioneers in the world of the atom. Our first concern is that this incredibly great force shall not be used for human destruction.

In 1946, when atomic power was still our monopoly, we sought through the Baruch plan such international control as would assure that atomic power would never be an instrument of war. The Soviet Union rejected that proposal. We nevertheless continue our efforts. President Eisenhower's atoms-for-peace proposal, made to the United Nations in 1953, finally led to positive results which should grow with time.

The International Atomic Energy Agency was established in 1957 with a present membership of 66 nations, including the U.S.S.R. But that government still fails to join to implement that vital part of the President's proposal which would have drawn down nuclear war stocks for peace stocks under international control.

We continue to press the Soviet Union in that respect.

We continue to develop and to spread the peaceful uses of atomic energy.

We have made bilateral agreements with 39 nations and have supplied research reactors to 16 nations. Negotiations are under way with others.

We are developing close and constructive relations with EURATOM, the atomic energy agency of six Western European nations.

We also give leadership in planning for the use of the new world of outer space. I recall President Eisenhower's letter of January 13, 1958, to Mr. Bulganin, where he said:

"I propose that we agree that outer space should be used only for peaceful purposes. We face a decisive moment in history in relation to this matter."

So far the Soviet reply has been evasive, but we feel confident that our viewpoint will prevail, if for no other reason than that the Soviet Union will finally see its own welfare in that result.

We look upon the north polar region as another changing area which should be organized for peace.

Mr. Khrushchev has pointed out to us that "the air route over the northern polar regions is the shortest distance between the U.S.S.R. and the U.S.A., and is therefore an important strategic area which has special significance in connection with the availability of rocket weapons."

That fact makes it the more imperative that these new routes of rapid communication shall be only peaceful and not carry threats leading to new fears, new armaments, and more "preparedness."

Our most intensive efforts are those designed to create a world where peace is stably ensconced.

(a) The United Nations is, of course, a primary reliance, and it has well served the cause for peace. Through the collective action of its members, aggression in

Korea was repelled. Through the United Nations, peace was restored in the Middle East.

We strive in all possible ways to invigorate the processes of the United Nations and have, under difficult circumstances, shown our loyalty to its principles. There are, however, built-in limitations.

The Soviet Union does not share the concepts of justice and of law which are enjoined upon the organization. It has "veto" power in the Security Council. Invoking a so-called "Principle of parity," it boycotts the General Assembly's Disarmament Commission because it cannot count upon enough votes on the Commission to control, at least negatively, its proceedings. Where the Soviet Union cannot legally block United Nations action, it flouts such actions as cross its will, as, for example, in the case of armed attack on Korea and on Hungary.

(b) Since the United Nations cannot dependably safeguard the peace, freedom, and independence of the nations, we must, and do, build elsewhere.

The United States has its own military establishment. This has two principal components. One is the Strategic Air Forces, so organized as to be able to wreck great destruction upon the Soviet Union should it initiate armed aggression against the United States or its allies. This is an effective deterrent to general war.

The United States has made cooperative defense treaties with 42 other nations. Further committals of United States power are authorized by the Formosa and Middle East resolutions.

The deterrent power of the United States thus acts as a shield to protect all nations with which we have or may make such arrangements. Senator Vandenberg, speaking in 1949 of the North Atlantic Treaty, said, "It spells out the conclusive warning that independent freedom is not an orphan in this western world, and that no armed aggression will have a chance to win." That warning has now been extended all around the globe, so as to eliminate the risk of miscalculations which have so often tempted military despots to "take a chance"—a chance which, in fact, often meant war.

The system of collective defense that the free nations have built is not one-sided. It is not just a United States gift to the world. Other nations contribute importantly. They provide bases which greatly increase the effectiveness of our deterrent power. They contribute the bulk of the ground forces. They provide, what is most important of all, a courageous will to resist powerful forces which often knock threateningly at their very doorstep.

This collective security system we are helping to build is no mere temporary expedient. It is a constructive evolution which should persist until it becomes possible to make the United Nations security processes both universal and dependable.

We see that the world of today requires better economic health than was tolerable in past times.

International trade is more than ever important. Our own foreign trade is now approximately $32.4 billion a year and provides employment to 4½ million of our farmers and workers. International trade is even more vital to the economic life of many other free-world countries.

A principal instrumentality and the outstanding symbol of our attitude to international trade is our Trade Agreements Act. The principle of this act was first adopted in 1934, and 10 times the Congress has acted to renew it. Any failure now to renew it would be a grave blow to the world's economy, including our own, and it could be fatal to security.

If the Soviet Union decides to use its increasing industrial productivity primarily to serve the goals of international communism, we may face acute problems.

It now stands to gain too much from the adverse impact on certain countries, as of Latin America, of rapidly shifting free-world prices and fluctuating free-world markets.

There is another type of danger if the Soviet state engages in ruthless competition with private free-world concerns which, to survive, must make a profit.

... we shall need to seek new initiatives to bring greater economic strength and unity. We shall be looking for the means to create a larger flow of private capital to the less developed countries, to make development assistance more effective, to bring about increased financial stability, and to cope with the serious problems which sometimes arise in commodity trade.

We are not content with a world where the potentials of destruction not only absorb vast economic effort but would, if unleashed, endanger all human life. So we strive for "disarmament," meaning measures of international inspection to diminish the danger of massive surprise attack and actual limitations or reductions of various types of armament. President Eisenhower's open-skies proposal of 1955 brought worldwide hope. But the Soviet Union has persistently evaded concrete inspection proposals.

The United States does not exclude the possibility of achieving significant agreements with the Soviet Union in certain areas of mutual interest. Within the past 5 years we have made several agreements with the Communists, notably the agreement that liberated Austria. But:

We do *not* believe that the "cold war" can be ended by a formula of words, so long as the basic creed of international communism requires world rule.

We do *not* believe that we should alter our position merely in reliance of Soviet promises. These have too often proved undependable. ...

We *do* believe that the Soviet Union, like the United States, would like to reduce the economic burden of modern armaments. We also believe that the Soviet Union, under present conditions, does not want war. Therefore, some common ground exists.

Chapter 17 SLOGANEERING: LIBERATION AND MASSIVE RETALIATION

LOUIS J. HALLE (1910-   ), a Professor at the Graduate Institute of International Studies in Geneva, Switzerland, since 1956, joined the Department of State in 1941 and became a member of the influential Policy Planning Staff established in 1947 by Secretary of State George Marshall in the Truman Administration. Halle resigned his post in 1954, partly because of the activities of Senator Joseph McCarthy. Halle wrote later that President Eisenhower and Secretary Dulles had acquiesced in "wrecking" the Foreign Service at this time because of domestic political pressures against appeasing Communism. Halle subsequently has written a number of books and articles on foreign policy, including The Nature of Power *(1955) and* Dream and Reality: Aspects of American Foreign Policy *(1959). His influential account of* The Cold War as History *views that struggle from a broad perspective. In this excerpt he inquires into the newness of the Eisenhower-Dulles ideas and raises questions about the influence of domestic politics upon foreign policies. He argues that Dulles, not Eisenhower, was in charge of affairs and that the Secretary's actions reveal his inexperience, moralism, and political motives. Thus Halle expresses concisely the liberal internationalist interpretation of foreign policy in the Eisenhower era.*

General Eisenhower was not himself an extremist, and he was far from inexperienced in foreign affairs. As a career officer he had always been politically neutral. . . . As a personality involved in national or international political situations, moreover, he had always displayed the virtues that go with a neutral disposition of mind. His greatest public usefulness had been as a conciliator of opposing factions, a harmonizer. During the War he had done a notable job of harmonizing the American and British military elements under his command, and he had done the same kind of job as a commander of NATO's international forces. When, in the late 1940's, rivalry between the American Army, Navy, and Air Force had reached a dangerous pitch, he was the man who was sent for to effect a reconciliation. It was

in situations like this that Eisenhower manifested his genius. The essential characteristic of any great harmonizer, however, is that he is himself detached in his view
of the issues in conflict. For if he had strong convictions of his own, on one side or
the other, he could not play the mediating role.

The neutrality of indifference that was native to Eisenhower's mind had been
strengthened by his training and experience as a general officer. He was at home
with staff procedures whereby an organized team of subordinates prepares the
decisions that the commanding officer then adopts as his own.

General Eisenhower, as the chosen leader of the Republican Party in the 1950's,
was a moderating influence among the extremists who had been rising through its
ranks. Taking his opinions, as always, from the environment in which he found
himself, he nevertheless spoke in terms of moderation himself, proclaiming principles that his Administration did not feel compelled to follow in practice. . . .

John Foster Dulles, who became Secretary of State in the Eisenhower Administration, was a New York lawyer of determined purpose who let nothing stand in the
way of its realization. His habit was to concentrate on one particular goal at a time,
and to concentrate on it so exclusively as to be genuinely incapable of comprehend-
ing, for the time being, any larger considerations. This made him unaware of the
sensibilities and interests of others, so that to the end he would remain a better
lawyer than he was a diplomat or statesman. From an early stage of his career he
had set himself to become Secretary of State. In pursuit of this goal he had cultivated a public legend of his competence in the field of international relations that
hid the actual paucity of his experience and the consequent limitations of his
knowledge. Given the respective characters of the President and his Secretary of
State, it is no wonder that American foreign policy under the Eisenhower Administration was identified more with the latter than with the former; so that, where one
had referred to Roosevelt's foreign policy or Truman's, one now referred to Dulles'
foreign policy.

The objective that Dulles set himself in the spring and summer of 1952, with his
usual single-mindedness, was a Republican victory in the Presidential elections
scheduled for November. One requirement of such success would be to assure the
country that a Republican Administration would, by boldness and purposeful
action, relieve it of the increasing frustration from which it had been suffering in
the Cold War, and particularly in the Korean War. . . . So Dulles . . . promised that
under the Republicans the Government would seize the initiative that the Democrats had allowed the Communists to retain. A Republican Administration, he said,
would see to it that it was Russia rather than the United States that found itself on
the defensive.

In this connection, Dulles denounced the containment policy of the Truman
Administration for its essential passivity. The Republicans, he promised, would
replace . . . containment by the objective of liberation. They would, specifically,

address themselves to the liberation of the East European nations and China from Moscow's grip. The plank on foreign policy that he wrote for the Republican platform said that a Republican victory would "mark the end of the negative, futile and immoral policy of 'containment' which abandons countless human beings to a despotism and Godless terrorism which in turn enables the rulers to forge the captives into a weapon for our destruction." In the ensuing campaign, both he and Eisenhower promised that under their Administration the Government would never rest until the peoples of East Europe had been restored to freedom. By "a policy of boldness" that wrested the initiative from Russia, the United States would achieve their liberation—albeit, as they always added, by peaceful means.

The containment policy had, from the beginning, been attacked for its essential passivity, which left the initiative to Moscow, and which also failed to foresee, in more explicit terms than those I have cited, any end to the necessity of continuing it along the frontier at which the opposing forces stood in 1947. In 1952, it was, therefore, eminently proper to ask what came after containment.

The proposed objective of liberation, however, as Dulles advanced it, raised questions of its own. Associated with the promise of a bold and dynamic policy, it aroused alarm that it would bring military force into play, detonating a third world war in which Western civilization would be finally consumed—in spite of Dulles' assurance that what he and Eisenhower proposed was the liberation of the captive nations by a moral and spiritual crusade, not a military crusade. (Especially in the first part of its career, the Eisenhower Administration would repeatedly declare its intention of achieving the national objectives abroad by means of the moral and spiritual power that the President and Secretary of State represented so outspokenly. The translation of this conception into reality, however, was never achieved. It was less effective in the foreign field than on the home scene, where the parable of the Pharisee and the Publican was not the best known chapter in the Bible.)

It must be understood, however, that when Dulles proclaimed the objective of liberation nothing was further from his mind than the international scene. He was concentrating exclusively on the domestic scene and on the objective of winning the forthcoming election. He had been deeply impressed by Samuel Lubell's analysis of the American political situation, *The Future of American Politics*, from which he had concluded that the Republicans could never win a national election unless they succeeded in detaching certain specific groups in the voting population from their normal Democratic allegiance Notable among such groups were Americans of East European descent concentrated in certain key industrial and urban areas. These groups, who still had relatives in the countries of their origin, or sentimental ties to them, would be moved to vote for the Party that promised to replace containment by liberation. Persons who were close to Dulles at the time . . . found that they could not get him to turn his mind from the electoral implications of liberation to its implications for the conduct of foreign affairs. When he became Secretary of State he would, at least in a perfunctory way, ask the bureaucracy under him to see what could be done to liberate the satellites by psychological devices. In fact, however, the new Administration, while continuing the policy of containment, would do nothing to put the proposed policy of liberation into effect.

Even after the Eisenhower Administration took office in January 1953 and Dulles became Secretary of State, the twenty-year habit of thinking only of the domestic scene persisted. The new Secretary concentrated on the objective of gaining for the new Administration, by appropriate words and attitudes, the confidence that its predecessor had lost; and he was prepared to go to the greatest lengths, by cultivating his own public image as the strong man of anti-Communism, to avoid the fate of Dean Acheson, who had disdained any such resort. This propensity on the part of Dulles explains certain difficulties that arose for him in his conduct of American foreign relations. It also explains, however, how he managed to retain the confidence and respect of the American public, regardless of those difficulties, until the day of his death in 1959—when the entire country mourned for the man who had, by his public attitudes, seemed such a tower of strength in the cause of Godliness and morality against Godless and immoral Communism.

The Republicans, more than the Democrats, thought in terms of a norm represented by the period . . . before the successive emergencies of World War I, the great depression, and World War II. These emergencies had perhaps required an abandonment of what they regarded as sound fiscal practices, just as an emergency in the career of an individual may require him temporarily to live beyond his income by borrowing. . . .Such lapses, however, must not be continued as a normal practice, and the dominant elements in the Republican Party were alarmed at the failure, so many years after World War II, to return to what President Harding . . . called "Normalcy."

The national budget, which had fallen to $32,289 million in Fiscal Year 1946-1947 (leaving a surplus of $754 million), had again risen, under the Truman Administration, to $73,982 million in 1952-1953 (leaving a deficit of over $900 million). For 1953-1954 the Truman Administration . . . had drawn up a budget of $78,587 million, and anticipated a deficit of $9,992 million. This sharp rise in expenditures and deficits represented, simply, the cost of containing Communism, of waging the Cold War. (Some three-quarters of President Truman's proposed budget for 1953-1954 was for . . . "national security programs," about 60% going directly to the armed services.)

The dilemma that confronted the new Republican Administration was clear. The only way it could move toward a balanced budget and, at the same time, lower taxes, was by a substantial reduction in military and related expenditures. (This was the more true because the preponderance of the other expenditures represented fixed charges for interest on the national debt and for veterans' programs.) It had, however, promised that it would adopt a much more aggressive and dynamic Cold War policy, by which it would put Russia on the defensive. How, its opponents asked, could it risk doing this at the same time that it was reducing the military strength of the United States?

Throughout 1953 there had been constant speculation, fed by hints from members of the Administration, that a new and better strategy, a "new look" in defense policy, was being prepared. There was no doubt that such a new strategy, if only for reasons of economy, would involve a more complete dependence on strategic nuclear power, thereby decreasing the requirements for American ground and naval forces. The anticipated "new look" aroused anxiety in Europe, where it was feared that the United States would drastically reduce its ground forces, if it did not withdraw them altogether.

Finally, on January 12, 1954, in an address delivered at the Council on Foreign Relations in New York, Secretary Dulles ostensibly presented . . . the new policy of the Administration. He began by observing that American policy hitherto had represented nothing more than a succession of responses to emergencies created by Russian initiative, and he implied that long-range planning had been neglected.

> The Soviet Communists [he said] are planning for what they call 'an entire historical era,' and we should do the same. They seek . . . gradually to divide and weaken the free nations by overextending them in efforts which, as Lenin put it, are 'beyond their strength, so that they come to practical bankruptcy.' Then, said Lenin, 'our victory is assured.' Then, said Stalin, will be 'the moment for the decisive blow.'

He referred to the need to avoid "military expenditures so vast that they lead to "practical bankruptcy," and added: "This can be done by placing more reliance on deterrent power and less dependence on local defensive power."

Referring to the previous inadequacy of policy and planning, he said that the new Administration had had to take "some basic policy decisions . . . to depend primarily upon a great capacity to retaliate, instantly, by means and at places of our choosing."

This last was the key sentence of an address that immediately aroused a storm of alarm and indignation throughout the Atlantic world. It was taken to mean that the United States was prepared to turn every local conflict into a worldwide nuclear war in which its allies, if not it as well, would be destroyed. The use of the word "instantly" was interpreted as meaning that the United States would not take the time to consult its allies before acting to transform a local conflict into Armageddon. Within hours of delivering the address the Secretary of State was a severely embarassed man. President Eisenhower felt compelled to deny, at his press-conference the next day, that any new "basic decision" on defense policy had been taken at all; and on March 17 he would deny that the so-called "new look" defense policy . . . was either new or revolutionary. Dulles, as was clear to anyone who knew the National Security Council document on which his address was based, had interpreted it to suit his own mind.

Ordinarily, when an important statement of policy is made on behalf of the Government of the United States, its text is prepared and checked in every phrase and nuance with the assistance of a corps of advisors. A fault of the Truman Administration, as we have seen, was to carry this . . . to the point where such statements lost the integrity and authority that depend on a single hand holding the pen. Dulles, up to January 12, 1954, had gone to the other extreme. Uncomfortable as he always was with the bureaucratic organization he had inherited, he had not known how to use it effectively. The "massive retaliation" speech, as it came to be known, was written entirely by him, and apparently with only one exception even the members of his immediate professional staff in the State Department did not know about it until it was delivered and published.

To this day, the "massive retaliation" speech is a poignant document purely as an expression of Dulles' personal character. There was always in him something of the little boy, who in his day-dreams, is the master-strategist, out-maneuvering and foiling his dastardly opponents at every turn by his boldness and craft. All his life he had cultivated a legend of himself based on this youthful day-dream, and now for the first time, at sixty-five years of age, he was in a position to realize it. . . . More than once it happened that he was unable to resist the temptation to strike public attitudes in fulfillment of this dream, attitudes that by their sheer exaggeration, provoked immediate public reactions highly embarassing to him. One such occasion was when he briefed a reporter who wanted material for an article about him for *Life* magazine. He told the reporter . . . that "the ability to get to the verge without getting into the war is the necessary art," whereupon he proceeded to illustrate the practice of this art by showing how the United States, since he had assumed his position as master mind in the conduct of its foreign relations, had done precisely this with brilliant effect on three separate occasions. Published as an interview, the public impression that the Secretary of State's boasting gave was of an immaturity and recklessness . . . that aroused widespread alarm through the alliance, just as the "massive retaliation" speech had two years earlier.

Chapter 18 EISENHOWER AND VIETNAM: A LIBERAL INTERPRETATION

THEODORE DRAPER *(1912-   ) has been
Research Fellow at the Hoover Institution on War,
Revolution and Peace since 1963 and a member of
the Institute for Advanced Studies at Princeton since
1968. He is the author of many books, including* The
Six Weeks War *(1944),* The Roots of American
Communism *(1957),* American Communism and
Soviet Russia *(1960),* Castro's Revolution *(1962) and*
The Dominican Revolt *(1968). In this excerpt from*
Abuse of Power *he raises the question: has the United
States deceived itself about Vietnam and the
American role there?*

The new Secretary of State, John Foster Dulles, recognized that as long as Indochina was nothing but a French colony, in fact if not in name, the United States did not have the political basis for all-out support of the Indochinese war. Under pressure from Dulles and French internal politics, the French government promised on July 3, 1953, "to perfect the independence and sovereignty" of the Associated States of Indochina, made up of Vietnam, Laos, and Cambodia. This declaration, which was never made good, gave Dulles the political basis to, as he put it, "underwrite the costs" of a new French military plan to defeat the Communists.

From June 1950 to May 1954, when the French were defeated at Dien Bien Phu, the United States provided $2.6 billion worth of military and economic aid to the French in Vietnam, no less than 80 percent of the total cost of the French war effort.

After the American investment in a French victory was made, American military and diplomatic leaders came to believe—or at least said publicly that they believed—in the likelihood of a French victory.

In May 1953 President Eisenhower and Secretary Dulles told Congress that United States aid would help "reduce this Communist pressure to manageable proportions." On December 2, 1953, Assistant Secretary of State for Far Eastern Affairs Walter S. Robertson assured an audience in New York that "the tide is now turning" in Indochina. In February 1954 Secretary of Defense Charles E. Wilson said that a French victory was "both possible and probable." In that same month Under Secretary of State Walter Bedell Smith reported: "The military situation in Indochina is favorable. . . . Tactically the French position is solid and the officers in the field seem confident of their ability to deal with the situation." In March 1954 Admiral Arthur W. Radford stated flatly, "The French are going to win." That same month, about six weeks before the French surrender at Dien Bien Phu, Secretary of State Dulles declared that he did "not expect that there is going to be a Communist victory in Indochina" and praised the French forces at Dien Bien Phu for "writing, in my opinion, a notable chapter in military history." When the American press reported French setbacks, Mr. Dulles accused American journalists of exaggeration and blamed them for attributing too much "importance" to the current Communist offensive. Asked about Communist "peace feelers," he brushed them off as lacking in "sincerity."

Thus, for the first time in American history, two Presidents, Truman and Eisenhower, and their respective Secretaries of State, Acheson and Dulles, enlisted the United States actively on the side of a colonial power—a total about-face from the Roosevelt position. From their point of view, of course, colonialism was preferable to communism. At best, then, the United States was faced with a choice of evils and could not win either way. The first step was, in many ways, typical of all the other steps. Dulles tried to get around the dilemma by arguing, as his successors proceeded to argue later in very different circumstances, that Ho Chi Minh's forces fraudulently purported to represent the cause of nationalism and independence but actually amounted to nothing more than an "arm of Communist aggression," directed, supplied, and equipped by the "Red masters of China." In this period, the American theory seemed to be that China was a satellite of Soviet Russia, and the North Vietnamese Communists were puppets of China. By making the Chinese the wire-pullers in Vietnam, Dulles sought to sidestep the issue of anti-colonialism and made the war against France a type of "foreign aggression," the foreigners in this case being the Chinese. It has been hard for later State Department officials to think of anything new or original after John Foster Dulles.

Despite Secretary of State Dulles' tortuous efforts to avoid the stigma of colonialism, one of the most severe judgments of American policy from 1946 to 1954 was made by Professor Frank N. Trager, an ardent supporter of post-1954 American intervention: "Throughout the long devastating years from the post-war return of the French in Indochina to Dien Bien Phu in 1954, the United States supported with incredible consistency the imperialists aims of France in Indochina." Even if Professor Trager may be doing some injustice to Secretary Dulles' attempts to get the French to make some commitment to Vietnamese independence, the fact remains that he was satisfied with words rather than with deeds, and even the words were too slippery for anyone to grasp.

. . . Vietnamese nationalism before 1954 was so heterogeneous that the Communists, though they were better organized and disciplined than any other group, were hardly the only alternative to French "imperialism." The Communists maneuvered themselves into increasingly advantageous positions precisely because the French administration was hostile to Vietnamese nationalism, not merely to the variety represented by the Communists. If the French, backed by the Americans, had wished to isolate the Communists from the other nationalist tendencies, the task would not have been beyond their joint resources and ingenuity. The American decision to support the French was all the more incongruous in view of the fact that, at this very time, the United States was urging, if not pressing, the British to get out of India and Burma and the Dutch to give up Indonesia.

Once France was defeated, however, American leaders professed not to be surprised and even to know the reason for the outcome. In his memoirs, President Dwight D. Eisenhower explained the French fiasco this way: "I am convinced that the French could not win the war because the internal political situation in Vietnam, weak and confused, badly weakened their military position." General Walter Bedell Smith, head of the American delegation to the Geneva Conference in 1954, which ended the Indochina war, told French Foreign Minister Georges Bidault that "any second-rate general should be able to win in Indochina if there were a proper political atmosphere." In 1965 Henry Cabot Lodge, then between his ambassadorships in Vietnam, cited General Smith's remarks as "one of the best things that any American has ever said about Indochina."

From all this it is clear that the United States would have been far better off in the late 1960s if its leaders had been as clairvoyant about their own problems in Vietnam as they had been about the French. For the American criticism of the French implicitly contained the indispensable ingredient for victory. That ingredient was essentially political in nature. If we may trust Generals Eisenhower and Smith, the formula for victory was a strong, clear internal Vietnamese political situation, a "proper political atmosphere." With that, even a second-rate general could win; without it, no first-rate general could win. If there was one lesson which the Americans should have learned from the French, and which they themselves said they had learned, it was that sound politics in Vietnam was the precondition of military victory, not that military victory was the precondition of sound politics.

The French defeat at Dien Bien Phu confronted the Eisenhower administration with a difficult and painful decision: Should the United States take the place of France in the Indochinese war?

Abstractly, Eisenhower and Dulles did not give themselves much choice. They were the first to apply the "domino theory" to Southeast Asia and even beyond. On April 7, 1954, President Eisenhower gave official status to what he then called the " 'falling domino' principle." It implied that the loss of Indochina would inevitably cause the fall of the rest of Southeast Asia like a "row of dominoes." Secretary Dulles tried to convince British Foreign Secretary Anthony Eden that the loss of Indochina would lead to the eventual loss of Thailand, Malaya, Burma, and Indonesia. This prospect seemed so alarming that leading figures in the Eisenhower administration advocated American military intervention in Vietnam to prevent it.

The outstanding "hawks" in 1953 and 1954 were Vice President Nixon, Secretary of State Dulles, and Admiral Radford. Nixon told the American Society of Newspaper Editors on April 16, 1954, that it was necessary to "take the risk now by putting our boys in" to avoid further Communist expansion in Asia and Indochina. Dulles also spoke publicly in favor of taking "serious risks." In March, Dulles told Eden, the United States Chiefs of Staff had suggested intervening in Vietnam with American naval and air forces. Even the possible use of atomic weapons, it is said, was raised in some fashion. According to General Matthew B. Ridgway, then the Army's Chief of Staff, "we very nearly found ourselves involved in a bloody jungle war in which our nuclear capability would have been almost useless." General Ridgway also recorded that "individuals of great influence, both in and out of government," raised the cry for United States intervention "to come to the aid of France with arms."

But the hawkish wing of the Administration met with determined opposition from at least three directions. Despite—or perhaps because of—his military background, President Eisenhower was most sensitive to Congressional approval of so serious a step as getting into an Asian war. In Congress the Nixon-Dulles-Radford line of military intervention encountered an extremely cold reception. Two of the most powerful and most conservative Senators came out strongly against an interventionist policy. One of them was Democratic Senator Richard B. Russell of Georgia, chairman of the key Armed Services Committee, a Southern patrician who was able to make or break both legislation and careers in the upper house. Later, Senator Russell recalled that he had been visited by Assistant Secretary of State Thruston B. Morton, who informed him of President Eisenhower's decision to assist the South Vietnamese. Senator Russell told Morton that he "feared this course would be costly in blood and treasure," though, once it was decided on, he "had no alternative but to support the flag." Another conservative Southern Senator who strongly opposed the Eisenhower decision on the Senate floor in 1954 was Democratic Senator John Stennis of Mississippi. According to Stennis, the first two hundred American Air Force mechanics, sent to South Vietnam early in 1954, were temporarily withdrawn as a result of Congressional objections. In his memoirs Eisenhower recalls that these two Senators were "uneasy about any American participation whatever," and he informed Secretary of State Dulles: "They fear that this may be opening the door to increased and unwise introduction of American troops into that area."

At a secret meeting on April 3, 1954, five senior Senators and three Representatives made known their apprehensions to Secretary Dulles and Admiral Radford. One of those who asked the most searching and embarrassing questions was the then Democratic Minority Leader, Senator Lyndon B. Johnson. He appeared to take the position that the United States could not intervene in Vietnam without allies and forced the Secretary of State to admit that he had not as yet even consulted them. Thus Lyndon Johnson's first important contribution to American policy in Vietnam tended to encourage restraint. Yet, with the fall of Dien Bien Phu the following month, Senator Johnson spoke publicly in quite another vein. He made the French defeat into the most "stunning reversal" ever suffered by American foreign policy "in all its history." He mourned that "we have been caught bluffing by our enemies" and had made our friends and Allies "frightened and wondering, as we do, where we are heading." The United States, he said, stood "in clear danger of being left naked and alone in a hostile world." Then, unaccountably, instead of advising his listeners to meet the danger in the world, he said that the prospect was so terribly painful "that we should turn our eyes from abroad and look homeward." It was, of course, a strictly partisan, rhetorical performance at a fund-raising dinner for his party in Washington, and only the fact that it was made by the future President in another Vietnamese crisis has invested it with any significance. Still, if this is what Senator Johnson thought of the responsibility that President Eisenhower bore for a *French* defeat, one wonders what Senator Johnson would have said of all the *American* setbacks and frustrations suffered by President Johnson.

After the April 3 meeting with the congressional leaders, however, Mr. Dulles did not give up so easily. He hit on the idea that he could sell his plan to Congress if he could make American intervention part of a larger "collective effort." For this purpose he needed the agreement and cooperation of Great Britain. On April 11, 1954, almost a month before the fall of Dien Bien Phu, Dulles went to London to convince Prime Minister Churchill and Foreign Secretary Eden. He tried out all the arguments which have become so familiar—the "domino theory" and historical analogies from the 1930s. The situation in Indochina, Dulles told Eden, "was analogous to the Japanese invasion of Manchuria in 1931 and to Hitler's reoccupation of the Rhineland." But Churchill and Eden refused to be persuaded. Churchill even saw through Dulles' game and confided to Eden that what the British "were being asked to do was to assist in misleading Congress into approving a military operation, which would in itself be ineffective, and might well bring the world to the verge of a major war."

Finally, opposition came from an unexpected quarter—the United States Army's high command, General Ridgway and General James M. Gavin, Chief of Plans and Development, took the position that the United States could hold on to Indochina, but that it was not worth the price that would have to be paid. An Army team of experts in every field was sent to Indochina to study the ramifications of a major intervention. The Army leaders, General Gavin related, projected the need for eight infantry divisions, plus about thirty-five engineer battalions. General Ridgway told Republican Senator George D. Aiken of Vermont that even if 2 million men were sent to Vietnam, they would "be swallowed up."

Thus the interventionist pressure from Vice President Nixon, Secretary of State Dulles, Admiral Radford, and others was more than offset by the reluctance of influential Senators, the disapproval of the British, and the misgivings of the Army command. This formidable opposition was too much for the innately prudent Eisenhower, whose most popular move was to get us out of one Asian war and who was now confronted with the demand to get us into another one. The line-up of forces was not lost on his Secretary of State.

Dulles was an extraordinarily artful diplomatist. He habitually reversed Theodore Roosevelt's advice about speaking softly and carrying a big stick. The Dulles method consisted of using strong words to hide inner weaknesses. He was a progenitor of the "domino theory," according to which a French defeat in Indochina would be fatal in the whole of Southeast Asia and beyond. Yet, when attempts were made to pin him down, he refused to subscribe to the full implications of his own theory. In order to make the "domino theory" inoperative, he expounded, it was only necessary to form a "collective-security arrangement" in Southeast Asia. Moreover, he added, "I do not want to give the impression either that if events that we could not control and which we do not anticipate should lead to their [the states of Indochina] being lost, that we would consider the whole situation hopeless, and we would give up in despair." On another occasion, on May 11, 1954, Dulles was specifically asked whether he thought the Southeast Asia area could be held without Indochina. He answered: "I do." This was not exactly orthodox "domino theory," but it served to give Dulles a safe line of retreat. Dulles succeeded in patching together a Southeast Asia Treaty Organization (SEATO)—composed of France, Britain, Australia, New Zealand, Thailand, the Philippines, Pakistan, and the United States—in September 1954, too late to prevent the French domino from falling in Indochina.

Once United States military intervention was doomed, Dulles hedged it about with so many conditions that he was in no danger of ever seeing it brought about. He propounded no fewer than five conditions as the necessary justification for intervention: (1) an invitation from the French; (2) clear assurance of complete independence to Laos, Cambodia, and Vietnam; (3) evidence of concern by the United Nations; (4) a collective effort on the part of other nations in the area; and (5) assurance that France would not itself withdraw from the battle until it was won. None of these conditions were, in the circumstances of 1954, likely to be completely satisfied, and Dulles would probably have added a few others if he had thought that these might be accepted.

The last American stand at the Geneva Conference was exquisitely Dullesian. First, Dulles professed to regard with holy horror any agreement which handed over more people and territory to a Communist regime. As a result, the United States refused to sign the Geneva Agreements. But then Under Secretary of State Bedell Smith was authorized to declare that the United States would "refrain from any threat or use of force to disturb" the agreements and "would view any renewal of the aggression in violation of the aforesaid agreements with grave concern and as seriously threatening international peace and security." After it was all over, though over eighteen million people of North Vietnam had been "handed over" to the Communists, President Eisenhower opined that the Geneva settlement had not been so bad after all; it was, he wrote in his memoirs, "the best" the French "could get under the circumstances" and he even "saw the beginning of development of better understanding between the Western powers and the nations of Southeast Asia." And Secretary Dulles later confided his thoughts about the agreements to a favorite American magazine; one of these was that handing over half of Vietnam to the Communists had actually "eliminated the possibility of a domino effect in Southeast Asia" by "saving" the other half, Laos and Cambodia. Finally, the United States looked on with favor, if nothing else, as Ngo Dinh Diem deliberately upset the Geneva applecart and defiantly repudiated the Geneva Agreements of 1955.

. . . the proponents of the 1954 "domino theory" were not prepared to think through and live up to their own doctrine. If, as President Eisenhower asserted, the French loss of Indochina would cause the fall of Southeast Asia "like a set of dominoes," and, as others did not fail to add, the fall of Southeast Asia would cause the loss of huge areas as far away as India, the stakes were so high that the advocates of this theory were obliged to take the most "serious risks," without the impossible conditions posed by Secretary Dulles. Not only did Eisenhower back away from the implications of his own theory but also the immediate consequences of the French defeat did not bear out his dire foreboding.

It is still important to keep in mind how the Indochinese war ended in 1954 because the story helps to explain the bitterness and doggedness of the Communists today. Ho Chi Minh made far-reaching concessions in the Geneva Agreements of July 1954, possibly under both Soviet and Communist Chinese pressure, as most authorities believe. Ho's victory over the French was decisive, but he agreed to take over only the northern half of the country, undoubtedly in the expectation that the

South, then in seeming chaos, would soon fall of its own accord into his hands. The Final Declaration of the Geneva Conference, a unique diplomatic instrument agreed to by all but signed by none, provided for general elections to unify the country in July 1956. Though there is reason to believe that no one, including the Communists, took this commitment very seriously, it gave the new regime in South Vietnam a breathing spell of two years. In short, the Communists have been fighting since 1954 to win back what they and everyone else thought they had already won. They had hardly intended to have Diem, who had contributed nothing to the victory over the French, reap its fruits. In 1954 Ho Chi Minh snatched compromise out of the jaws of victory; today the United States is afraid that he will snatch victory out of the jaws of compromise. In any case, this odd background makes Vietnam idiosyncratic in Communist bids for power. It is hard to imagine the same chain of events elsewhere.

President Eisenhower's "solution" in 1954 was a compromise between extremes—one demanding full military intervention, the other complete abstention. To the question which side it was on, the Eisenhower administration answered unequivocally—it was for Ngo Dinh Diem. He took office as Prime Minister under Emperor Bao Dai—who had worked for the French, the Japanese, the Communists, and again the French—just before the Geneva Agreements of July 1954 brought to an end the war waged by the Vietnamese Communists against French colonial rule. Diem, a long-time exile, had not taken part in this struggle but had stayed in the United States for a period before the French collapse, making friends in high places and impressing a variety of Americans, official and unofficial, that he was a man of nationalist convictions and progressive ideas. While Ngo Dinh Diem became the first Vietnamese instrument of American policy, he was far from being the first choice of the Vietnamese themselves. Of all the things Mr. Eisenhower has regretted putting down on paper, the list may well be topped by the admission in his memoirs that all knowledgeable persons at the time agreed that "had elections been held as of the time of the fighting, possibly 80 per cent of the population would have voted for the Communist Ho Chi Minh as their leader rather than Chief of State Bao Dai." He might also have said rather than Ngo Dinh Diem, who at first merely seemed to represent the Bao Dai regime. As late as 1965, Senator Russell said that Ho could have won again.[1]

I do not cite these statements as evidence of how democratic Ho Chi Minh would have been. He might have taken power democratically, but he would not have kept power democratically, which is far more important. In 1960 the "elections" in North Vietnam resulted in a 99.8 per-cent majority for the ruling Communist Party and its two small satellite groups, with no one permitted to run on an opposition platform. For this reason it is fatuous to imagine that Vietnam would have been more "democratic" if Ho Chi Minh had been permitted to get an 80-per-cent majority in a national election, as provided for by the Geneva Agreements. The only reason for citing Eisenhower's statement is that it underlines the unique character of the Vietnam problem. In what other country could a Communist leader have been assured of anything close to an 80-per-cent sweep in a free election.

But the Eisenhower administration made far more a political and economic than a military commitment. The American gamble was held down by the understanding that the United States was willing to help Diem's regime only if it proved capable of helping itself. On October 23, 1954, President Eisenhower sent Prime Minister Diem a letter in which he explicitly stated the conditional nature of this support. The American aid program was contemplated, the letter said, "provided that your Government is prepared to give assurances as to the standards of performance it would be able to maintain in the event such aid were supplied." The American offer, it went on, was intended to make the government of Vietnam "a strong viable state, capable of resisting attempted subversion or aggression through military means. The Government of the United States expects that this aid will be met by performance on the part of the Government in Vietnam in undertaking needed reforms." Yet this letter has been cited as if it were an unconditional "commitment" on the part of the United States "to resist Communist aggression" from then to the present and seemingly for all time. It should also be noted that the letter put the burden of resistance on the government of Vietnam, not on the United States. On June 2, 1964, President Johnson said that "our commitment today is just the same as the commitment made by President Eisenhower to President Diem in 1954—a commitment to help these people help themselves." If so, it is still nothing more than an offer of aid conditional on "the standards of performance" of, and "needed reforms" by, the government of South Vietnam. The Eisenhower policy was one of limited liability and, in principle, it set the pattern until 1965.

For our purposes, the main thing to note is that, in the end, the main reason given by the Americans, from President Eisenhower to Senator John F. Kennedy, for the French defeat was political. The French could not win, as President Eisenhower put it, as long as the internal political situation in Vietnam was "weak and confused." This is no less true of the United States, with the addition of something else, for which the French were not strong enough: our military position has been strengthened every time the internal political situation in Vietnam has weakened.

Chapter 19 DULLES AND THE SUEZ CRISIS

ROSCOE DRUMMOND *(1902-   ) was for many years a reporter and then editor of the* Christian Science Monitor. *He was chief of the Washington Bureau of the New York* Herald-Tribune *during the 1950's and is now Washington columnist for the Los Angeles* Times *syndicate.* GASTON COBLENTZ *was the* Herald-Tribune's *foreign correspondent in Bonn, Germany, during the 1950's. Drummond and Coblentz were basically in sympathy with Dulles' views of foreign relations but were not uncritical. In this excerpt they analyze Dulles' role in the Suez crisis of 1956. How did the United States and Great Britain, old friends and allies come into conflict with each other?*

A future historian writing a charitable account of the roles of Dulles and Eden in the Suez disaster will say that a complete misunderstanding prevailed between the two as to the nature and purpose of each other's actions. . . .

By the time the Suez crisis exploded in mid-1956, their antagonism had reached a point at which both men staged artificial displays of friendliness to conceal their reciprocal enmity.

During their meetings in London and Washington it was, on the surface, virtually impossible to discern the underlying hostility. . . .

By early 1956, six months before Nasser seized the Suez Canal, Eden is known to have been commonly using the epithet "that terrible man" in speaking of Dulles.

Roscoe Drummond and Gaston Coblentz, *Duel at the Brink: John Foster Dulles' Command of American Power* (Garden City, N. Y., 1960), pp. 161-163, 169-178. Reprinted by permission of Roscoe Drummond and Gaston Coblentz.

Dulles, in turn, was known by his closest associates in Washington and New York to rarely be happy with Eden as an ally against the Kremlin. He became wary of Eden adopting mediatory tactics when tension mounted between the United States and the Communists. He considered that Foreign Office vanity played a role in Eden's diplomatic make-up. Further, he was not always impressed by Eden's professional homework. Dulles expected others to be as diligently briefed as he was and could be acrimonious when they were not.

There is no truth to the view that Dulles was anti-British. He made clear to his associates and to his ambassadors in Europe . . . that he considered the Anglo-American alliance as a keystone of his foreign policy.

There were, however, underlying differences between his fundamental approach to the Cold War and that which he felt he detected in London. He said he found the British too inclined to regard the Soviet government as another imperialistic Russian regime along traditional lines, with whom one could do business as one had done with the Czars.

This attitude towards the Kremlin, Dulles felt, colored British tactics toward Western Europe. He saw it as permitting London to maneuver against Franco-German federation rather than joining him in promoting it as a barrier against Soviet Communism.

The seeds of the fiasco were planted in early 1956 when Eden revised his basic approach toward Nasser from one of support to one of hostility. Previously, two conflicting attitudes toward the Egyptian dictator had prevailed in the British cabinet. One group, including Eden, had favored cultivating him, The other . . . craved to eliminate him from the Middle Eastern scene.

After Foreign Secretary Selwyn Lloyd was stoned by Nasser agents in Bahrein, the entire cabinet finally swung to a policy of seeking Nasser's removal.

. . . . as late as December, 1955, ten months before Britain's attack on Suez, Eden had been urging Washington to subsidize Nasser's huge Aswan Dam project. Britain was also going to contribute a sizeable sum. But, by the spring of 1956, Eden had changed his mind, and was urging Washington not to pay for it.

A few weeks later, Dulles finally withdrew the United States' Aswan offer in a calculatedly offensive manner. By this action Dulles touched off Nasser's seizure of the Suez Canal and the violent events which followed. However, the move was in substance precisely what had been urged by Eden. . . .

Moreover, Dulles had privately informed Eden and Lloyd that the American move was imminent. . . . Henry Cabot Lodge . . . told [Britain's UN delegate Anthony] Nutting that Dulles had made up his mind to act . . . there was the prospect of a serious rebuff from Congress in a presidential election year if the

Eisenhower Administration sought to go ahead. . . . Eden immediately followed suit by announcing the withdrawal of Britain's Aswan aid offer less than twenty-four hours after Dulles had acted. Eden's move was scarcely calculated to soften the blow.

This set of circumstances, coupled with the events that rapidly ensued, gave Dulles an impression that Eden was secretly almost pleased by Nasser's retaliatory seizure of Suez. Dulles soon gained the belief that Eden actually welcomed Nasser's retaliation as furnishing an opportunity for Britain to strike back by invading Egypt. According to high-ranking members of Sir Anthony's entourage . . . Dulles' impression was not entirely unjustified.

. . . . Dulles had been obliged to give a high priority to domestic politics in withdrawing the Aswan offer. Congress had just dealt two sharp blows to the Eisenhower Administration. The first was a large slash in the current foreign aid bill. The second was an unwanted increase in the military appropriations allotment, by the identical amount. . . . Congress was plainly not in a mood to make a $56,000,000 first-installment investment in Nasser's dam.

The Egyptian leader, then at his most ambitious, had been flaunting neutralism in its most offensive form. He had . . . established diplomatic relations with Communist China a few days before Congress was scheduled to act on Aswan.

In addition, Nasser was for Dulles at that moment the standard-bearer of the "immoral" Khrushchev-promoted neutralist tide spreading through the Afro-Arab-Asian world. Moreover, Nasser was steadily buying more weapons from Moscow. Aswan furnished Dulles a made-to-order occasion to demonstrate that the United States would bestow its aid on friends rather than on those who would not see the difference between good and evil. . . . he chose the day that the Egyptian leader . . . had instructed Cairo's Ambassador in Washington to call at the State Department and accept the terms of the Aswan aid offer. No sooner had the envoy left the Department than Dulles curtly announced that the American offer was withdrawn.

France's alarmed envoy to Washington, Couve de Murville, a Middle Eastern expert and subsequently de Gaulle's Foreign Minister, rushed to warn the State Department that Nasser would retaliate, probably by seizing the Canal. The French, with the British, were the principal interested parties in the Suez Canal Company. The French Ambassador is known to have been astounded by what appeared to him to be an incomprehending attitude at the Department. During the next twenty-four hours, other foreign envoys in Washington gained a similar impression that Dulles had simply failed to foresee a seizure of the Canal. Dulles later blandly asserted that Nasser had planned to seize the Canal anyway.

Nasser's blow at one of the holiest remnants of European imperialism came exactly a week later. Suez instantly became the acid test of British and French power in the postwar world.

The friction-ridden Dulles-Eden relationship suddenly took a new, even more exacerbating form. Eden had previously been playing the would-be mentor and restrainer of the Dulles of rollback and massive retaliation. Suddenly, Dulles was cast as . . . restrainer of an Eden plotting a nineteenth-century-vintage military attack on Egypt. This reversal of roles further aggravated the relationship.

Dulles embarked on what proved to be a fatally ineffective course. He played Eden along from week to week, for more than a month. On three successive flights to London, he tried to gain time until Eden's resolve to attack Egypt might weaken. He let Eden gain the impression that Washington would not oppose an Anglo-French invasion if all the attempts at negotiation failed. When closeted with Eden, he gave the impression of being at one with him in his aversion to Nasser. In public, however, he infuriated Eden by pointedly disassociating the United States from British colonialism.

One of his main time-gaining devices was a legalistically skillful proposal for a multi-national Suez Canal Users Association. However, Eden immediately seized on it as an instrument for bringing drastic pressure to bear on Nasser, including the threat of force. Dulles, seeking Eden's adherence to the proposal, ambiguously tolerated this interpretation. This, in turn, encouraged Eden to believe the United States would . . . acquiesce in draconic action against Nasser. However, it rapidly emerged that Dulles was unwilling to put the kind of teeth into the plan which even the most moderate members of the Eden government demanded. . . .

Dulles continued to talk indignantly of Nasser's seizure of the Canal. But, when the chips were down, he not only flatly opposed military action but refused to back Eden in massive economic pressure. . . . Even this was too close an association for Dulles with the remnants of British imperialism.

Eden's reaction was embittered. To him, Dulles' performance . . . became another piece of "Dulles trickery."

Meanwhile, Eden cast aside the cloak of polished British diplomacy. . . . With wild inaccuracy, he began likening Nasser to Adolf Hitler. British propaganda . . . attempted to market the White-Man's-Burden precept that Egypt would be hopelessly incapable of operating the Canal. . . . British ambassadors in Europe spread the word that force might be necessary to restore decent respect for international law in Cairo.

By this time, effective communication between Dulles and Eden, and between Washington and London, had begun to break down. The two great partners . . . were acting like hostile parties in a bitter law suit. As a result, there was little diplomatic traffic between the two capitals during the crisis' final crescendo just before the Anglo-French-Israeli attack. Further embittered by Dulles' equivocation on the Canal Users' plan, Eden decided that from there on, the less said to Dulles, the better.

Then came the Eden ultimatum to Nasser . . . and the incompetent British military operation that followed. At this point Eisenhower, rather than Dulles, made the climactic series of telephone calls to Eden that brought the attack to a halt. . . .

On the fourth day, the eve of the Port Said landing, Dulles was rushed to Walter Reed Hospital. . . . But, despite his immense role in world affairs, the illness was overshadowed by . . . the invasion of Egypt, the American presidential elections, and the Soviet Army's savage suppression of the Hungarian revolt.

Eisenhower dealt with 10 Downing Street directly on the telephone. . . . his language was that of extreme tension and irritation rather than outright rudeness, as then believed.

Eden . . . was the only member of the British cabinet who still wanted to continue the attack when the cabinet met later that day. He was voted down by 17 to 1. The opposition to him included Foreign Secretary Selwyn Lloyd [and] . . . agreed on one point: Britain could not go on.

Dulles had seen that the run on the pound sterling in world financial markets was proving a powerful lever on London, and visibly refrained from coming to the rescue. Precipitous international pressure on the pound was threatening the British economy with catastrophe.

New pressure on sterling from American quarters weighed far more heavily in London than either the world's moral opprobrium or Moscow's sudden threat to devastate the British Isles with rockets.

Dulles' opposition to the Suez attack was ultimately to bulk large in the regeneration of his battered name. It proved to many that when he condemned aggression, he did not mean solely Soviet aggression. It proved to skeptics that there was more to Dulles than sanctimonious anti-Communist rhetoric. But its immediate effect was to unleash in Britain, France, and in many American quarters an anti-Dulles clamor that brought his reputation to its nadir. He was pilloried as a maladroit failure who was not only unable to cope with Khrushchev but who was, to boot, wrecking the Western allaince.

. . . six weeks after Suez, Dulles flew to Paris for a NATO meeting. . . . He had a long and revealing talk with France's Foreign Minister [Christian] Pineau on Washington's break with its oldest friends over Suez. . . .

Dulles began by explaining to Pineau that the United States had lost confidence in Nasser during the months before withdrawal of the Aswan aid offer, and that American opposition to the attack on Egypt was accordingly not based on a desire to keep Nasser in power.

But, Dulles said, American acquiescence in the Anglo-French-Israeli invasion would have deprived Washington of its strongest arguments in restraining Chiang

Kai-shek on Formosa and Syngman Rhee in Korea from aggressive military action against the Communists.

Moreover, he said, it would have made it more difficult to deter the nationalist forces in West Germany. Lastly, he said, it would have encouraged minority groups in the United States to urge military action to liberate the Eastern European satellites. . . .

Dulles contended that failure by the United States to halt the Suez invasion would thus have led to proliferating military conflicts. The inevitable result, he said, would have been the holocaust of World War III.

He then reverted to Nasser. He said it was clear that the United States did not accord preference to Nasser or the Arabs over Britain and France, its traditional and great allies. He noted that neither cultural nor racial ties bound the United States to the Arabs. But, he said, the use of force against Egypt could only result in rallying popular support behind Nasser.

The United States would be glad to see Nasser replaced, Dulles said, but it would have to stem from "the necessary internal conditions." By this, the French understood Dulles to mean an overthrow of Nasser by underground methods.

When [French Prime Minister Guy] Mollet and Pineau arrived in Washington for the post-Suez Franco-American conciliation talks, the atmosphere was cordial. . . .

However, Pineau found Dulles excessively irritable toward the Israelis, whom Washington was then intensely pressuring to evacuate the Gaza Strip.

Dulles told Pineau that the Israelis were not supple enough in their diplomacy, and that they reacted too brusquely to every development.

"I told Dulles that he was not putting himself in the Israelis' position. Perhaps the one main criticism to be made of Dulles [said Pineau later] is that he often did not put himself in other people's shoes. . . ."

Chapter 20 THE MILITARY-INDUSTRIAL COMPLEX

PRESIDENT EISENHOWER *bade farewell to the American people in a radio and television address on January 17, 1961. He spoke of keeping peace in the world and balance among government programs inside the United States. Most listeners were startled by his warning that a new "military-industrial complex" might endanger liberty and democratic processes. How is it that a military man, expecially one regarded as a passive President, could utter such a warning? At a news conference the next day President Eisenhower added a comment that raises further questions about the purposes of government and power.*

We now stand ten years past the midpoint of a century that has witnessed four major wars among great nations. Three of these involved our own country. Despite these holocausts, America is today the strongest, the most influential and most productive nation in the world. Understandably proud of this pre-eminence, we yet realize that America's leadership and prestige depend, not merely upon our unmatched material progress, riches and military strength, but on how we use our power in the interests of world peace and human betterment.

Throughout America's adventure in free government, our basic purposes have been to keep the peace; to foster progress in human achievement, and to enhance liberty, dignity and integrity among people and among nations. To strive for less would be unworthy of a free and religious people. Any failure traceable to arro-

Public Papers of the Presidents of the United States: Dwight D. Eisenhower, 1960-1961 (Washington, 1961), pp. 1036-1040, 1045.

gance, or our lack of comprehension or readiness to sacrifice would inflict upon us grievous hurt both at home and abroad.

Crises there will continue to be. In meeting them, whether foreign or domestic, great or small, there is a recurring temptation to feel that some spectacular and costly action could become the miraculous solution to all current difficulties. A huge increase in newer elements of our defense; development of unrealistic programs to cure every ill in agriculture; a dramatic expansion in basic and applied research—these and many other possibilities, each possibly promising in itself, may be suggested as the only way to the road we wish to travel.

But each proposal must be weighed in the light of a broader consideration: the need to maintain balance in and among national programs—balance between the private and the public economy, balance between cost and hoped for advantage— balance between the clearly necessary and the comfortably desirable; balance between our essential requirements as a nation and the duties imposed by the nation upon the individual; balance between actions of the moment and the national welfare of the future. Good judgment seeks balance and progress; lack of it eventually finds imbalance and frustration.

The record of many decades stands as proof that our people and their government have, in the main, understood these truths and have responded to them well, in the face of stress and threat. But threats, new in kind or degreee, constantly arise. I mention two only.

A vital element in keeping the peace is our military establishment. Our arms must be mighty, ready for instant action, so that no potential aggressor may be tempted to risk his own destruction.

Our military organization today bears little relation to that known by any of my predecessors in peacetime, or indeed by the fighting men of World War II or Korea.

Until the latest of our world conflicts, the United States had no armaments industry. American makers of plowshares could, with time and as required, make swords as well. But now we can no longer risk emergency improvisation of national defense; we have been compelled to create a permanent armaments industry of vast proportions. Added to this, three and a half million men and women are directly engaged in the defense establishment. We annually spend on military security more than the net income of all United States corporations.

This conjunction of an immense military establishment and a large arms industry is new in the American experience. The total influence—economic, political, even spiritual—is felt in every city, every State house, every office of the Federal government. We recognize the imperative need for this development. Yet we must not fail to comprehend its grave implications. Our toil, resources and livelihood are all involved; so is the very structure of our society.

In the councils of government, we must guard against the acquisition of unwarranted influence, whether sought or unsought, by the military-industrial complex. The potential for the disastrous rise of misplaced power exists and will persist.

We must never let the weight of this combination endanger our liberties or democratic processes. We should take nothing for granted. Only an alert and knowledgeable citizenry can compel the proper meshing of the huge industrial and military machinery of defense with our peaceful methods and goals, so that security and liberty may prosper together.

Akin to, and largely responsible for the sweeping changes in our industrial-military posture, has been the technological revolution during recent decades.

In this revolution, research has become central; it also becomes more formalized, complex, and costly. A steadily increasing share is conducted for, by, or at the direction of, the Federal government.

Today, the solitary inventor, tinkering in his shop, has been overshadowed by task forces of scientists in laboratories and testing fields. In the same fashion, the free university, historically the fountainhead of free ideas and scientific discovery, has experienced a revolution in the conduct of research. Partly because of the huge costs involved, a government contract becomes virtually a substitute for intellectual curiosity. For every old blackboard there are now hundreds of new electronic computers.

The prospect of domination of the nation's scholars by Federal employment, project allocations, and the power of money is ever present—and is gravely to be regarded.

Yet, in holding scientific research and discovery in respect, as we should, we must also be alert to the equal and opposite danger that public policy could itself become the captive of a scientific-technological elite.

It is the task of statesmanship to mold, to balance, and to integrate these and other forces, new and old, within the principles of our democratic system—ever aiming toward the supreme goals of our free society.

Down the long lane of the history yet to be written America knows that this world of ours, ever growing smaller, must avoid becoming a community of dreadful fear and hate, and be, instead, a proud confederation of mutual trust and respect.

Such a confederation must be one of equals. The weakest must come to the conference table with the same confidence as do we, protected as we are by our moral, economic, and military strength. That table, though scarred by many past frustrations, cannot be abandoned for the certain agony of the battlefield.

Disarmament, with mutual honor and confidence, is a continuing imperative. Together we must learn how to compose differences, not with arms, but with intellect and decent purpose. Because this need is so sharp and apparent I confess that I lay down my official responsibilities in this field with a definite sense of disappointment. As one who has witnessed the horror and the lingering sadness of war—as one who knows that another war could utterly destroy this civilization which has been so slowly and painfully built over thousands of years—I wish I could say tonight that a lasting peace is in sight.

Happily, I can say that war has been avoided. Steady progress toward our ultimate goal has been made. But, so much remains to be done. As a private citizen, I shall never cease to do what little I can to help the world advance along that road.

The President's News Conference of January 18, 1961

Q. Mr. President, last night you called attention to the danger that public policy could become the captive of a scientific technological elite. What specific steps would you recommend to prevent this?

The President. I know nothing here that is possible, or useful, except the performance of the duties of responsible citizenship. It is only a citizenry, an alert and informed citizenry which can keep these abuses from coming about. And I did point out last evening that some of this misuse of influence and power could come about unwittingly but just by the very nature of the thing. When you see almost every one of your magazines, no matter what they are advertising, has a picture of the Titan missile or the Atlas or solid fuel or other things, there is becoming a great influence, almost an insidious penetration of our own minds that the only thing this country is engaged in is weaponry and missiles. And, I'll tell you we just can't afford to do that. The reason we have them is to protect the great values in which we believe, and they are far deeper even than our own lives and our own property, as I see it.

Guide to Further Reading

The contemporary moods and intellectual perspectives of the Eisenhower Era are as important as its politics, to which they are intimately related. The Second World War, the subsequent international crises, and the new domestic prosperity helped to shape the period's dominant views, dubbed "consensus" thinking because of the marked emphasis on the shared principles and distinctive features of American life. Some of the most sophisticated and *influential expressions of consensus* thought are to be found in the writings of such historians as Richard Hofstadter, *The American Political Tradition* (New York, 1948); Daniel Boorstin, *The Genius of American Politics* (Chicago, 1953); David Potter, whose work is excerpted in this volume; and other scholars who range in subject field and political perspective from Rowland Berthoff and Edmund S. Morgan to William A. Williams. Scholars reflecting on the vogue of consensus have tended to give most extended attention to the historians, somewhat neglecting comparable and equally seminal trends in political science, sociology, and other areas of thought; students of the intellectual climate of the 1950's should become familiar with the writings of Louis Hartz, Robert Dahl, Seymour Lipset, V. O. Key, Herbert McCloskey, and Will Herberg, as well as with David Riesman and Daniel Bell, whose writings are incorporated in this book. Noteworthy early commentaries on consensus include John Higham, "Beyond Consensus: The Historian as Moral Critic," *The American Historical Review*, LXVII (April, 1962), 609-625, and J. Rogers Hollingsworth, "Consensus and Continuity in Recent American Historical Writing," *South Atlantic Quarterly*, 61 (Winter, 1962), 40-50.

The vital pulse of the 1950's may also be felt in the *journalism* of the period, particularly in publications that were alert to significant social and economic change. *Fortune* published numerous readable and perceptive articles, such as the series on the "transient" business executives by William H. Whyte, Jr., in vols. 47-48 (May, June, and July, 1953), and "Are Cities Un-American?" by the same author in vol. 56 (September, 1957). See also the widely popular volume by Whyte, *The Organization Man* (New York, 1956), and as Editors of Fortune, *U.S.A., The Permanent Revolution* (New York, 1951), and *The Changing American Market* (New York, 1955).

Among the many useful *contemporary sociological studies* are Sylvia Fava, "Suburbanism as a Way of Life," *American Sociological Review*, 21 (February, 1956), 34-36; Ely Chinoy, "Social Mobility Trends," *ibid.*, 20 (April, 1955), 180-186; Natalie Rogoff, *Recent Trends in Occupational Mobility* (Glencoe, 1953); Mabel Newcomer, *The Big Business Executive* (New York, 1955); W. Lloyd Warner and James Abegglen, *Big Business Leaders in America* (New York, 1955); James A. Kahl, *The American Class Structure* (New York, 1957); Reinhard Bendix and Seymour Lipset, *Class, Status, and Power* (Glencoe, 1953); and Bruce Bliven (ed.), *Twentieth Century Unlimited* (Philadelphia, 1950), as well as books by David Riesman, C. Wright Mills, and others excerpted in this volume. Daniel Bell (ed.), *The New American Right* (New York, 1955) and the popular account by Samuel Lubell, *The Future of American Politics* (New York, 1951), lead the reader into the politics of the period.

Economists also provided influential contemporary appraisals, some of which contributed to the consensus perspective. These include David Lilienthal, *Big Business: A New Era* (New York, 1953): Adolph A. Berle, Jr., *The Twentieth Century Capitalist Revolution* (New York, 1954), in which it is argued that the nature of corporations had changed; and John Kenneth Galbraith, *American Capitalism* (Boston, 1952), in which the writer contended that a countervailing balance of government, business, and labor shaped the post-New Deal economy. Galbraith, evolving towards a New Frontiersman, later wrote iconoclastically of *The Affluent Society* (Boston, 1958) which neglected the public good. Simon Kuznets, however, revealed significant shifts downward in the *Shares of Upper Incomes Groups in Income and Savings* (New York, 1953). On labor, see C. Wright Mills, *The New Men of Power* (New York, 1956); and Jack Barbash, *The Practice of Unionism* (New

York, 1956); on agriculture, Murray Benedict, *Farm Policies of the United States* (New York, 1953), and Benedict and O. C. Stine, *The Agricultural Commodity Programs* (New York, 1956). The contemporary value of the American dollar was made graphic by Charles P. Kindleberger, *The Dollar Shortage* (Boston, 1950). William A. Brown and Redvers Opie, *American Foreign Assistance* (Washington, 1953), is a valuable account of foreign-aid programs meant to remedy international economic problems.

A volume in the *American Problem Studies* edited by Arnold M. Paul, *Black Americans and the Supreme Court Since Emancipation* (New York, 1972), effectively treats issues of *law and civil rights*. Louis Harlan, *The Negro in American History* (Washington, 1965), is a useful guide. J. Saunders Redding, *The Lonesome Road* (Garden City, 1958), and David Tyack, *Nobody Knows* (New York, 1969), are readable overviews, while John Hope Franklin, *From Slavery to Freedom* (New York, 1956), is detailed. Louis Lomax, *The Negro Revolt* (New York, 1962), surveys change after 1955.

Bernard Rosenberg and David M. White (eds.), *Mass Culture* (Glencoe, 1957), is largely hostile. Harry R. Huebel (ed.), *Things in the Driver's Seat* (Chicago, 1972), contains lively readings on popular culture in the 1950's. See also George R. Stewart, *American Ways of Life* (Garden City, 1954) and Leslie Fiedler, *An End to Innocence* (Boston, 1955). Norman Mailer, "The White Negro," *Advertisements for Myself* (New York, 1959), was a "beat" manifesto.

Lawrence A. Cremin, *The Transformation of the School* (New York, 1961), provides a context for understanding the numerous critics of American *public education* in the 1950's, including Albert Lynd, Mortimer Smith, Arthur Bestor, and James B. Conant. Robert M. MacIver, *Academic Freedom in Our Time* (New York, 1955) addressed the crisis in higher education related to McCarthyism.

Ihab Hassan, *Radical Innocence* (Princeton, 1961), is an early analysis of *the era's literature*. Sam Hunter, *Modern American Painting and Sculpture* (New York, 1959), is a knowledgeable if sometimes opaque introduction to the new visual arts.

Conservative thought of the era is expressed in Richard Weaver, *Ideas Have Consequences* (Chicago, 1948); Peter Viereck, *Conservatism Revisited* (New York, 1959); R. A. Nisbet, *The Quest for Community* (New York, 1953); and various books by Russell Kirk, as well as by the provocative young journalist William F. Buckley, Jr., and European scholars who taught in America, including Friedrich Hayek and Leo Strauss. Ronald Lora, *Conservative Minds in America* (Chicago, 1971), provides an analysis.

Adlai Stevenson articulated *liberal thinking* in *Call to Greatness* (New York, 1954), and *The New America* (New York, 1957). See also the writings of such journalists as Murray Kempton, *America Comes of Middle Age* (Boston, 1963), and Richard H. Rovere, *Senator Joe McCarthy* (New York, 1960), a highly critical account. The school of "realism" in the study of international affairs is represented by Hans Morgenthau, Robert E. Osgood, Bernard Brodie, Herman Kahn, and

George F. Kennan, whose *American Diplomacy, 1900-50* (Chicago, 1951), became a bible in many history and political-science classes in the 1950's. The influence of these writers on policy, however, was perhaps greater after 1961. A convenient guide to these ideas is Urs Schwarz, *American Strategy* (New York, 1967).

The literature on the Eisenhower Administration reflects the same contemporary moods as well as partisanship and a maturing historical perspective. During the 1950's and for a decade thereafter some academic writers, social critics and journalists attacked the President and his administration for weakness in leadership and for failing to act decisively in domestic and international affairs. The President had his ardent defenders, and in recent years a few "revisionist" accounts have appeared.

A number of primary sources have also been published. Of particular importance are *Public Papers of the Presidents of the United States: Dwight D. Eisenhower, 1953-1961* (Washington, D. C., 1958-1961), containing speeches and press conferences; *The Department of State Bulletin* for 1953-1961 (vols. 28 through 44), containing speeches and press conferences of Secretaries Dulles and Herter and of other prominent diplomats as well as important documents; *Documents on American Foreign Relations*, published annually by the Council on Foreign Relations; *The Pentagon Papers: The Senator Gravel Edition* (Boston, 1971), Vol. 1 containing National Security Council documents, minutes of meetings, Joint Chiefs of Staff recommendations and other important material. Also useful are: Robert L. Branyan and Lawrence H. Larsen, eds., *The Eisenhower Administration, 1953-1961: A Documentary History* (2 vols., New York, 1971); Rudolph L. Treuenfels, ed., *Eisenhower Speaks* (New York, 1948), containing messages and speeches from V-E Day in 1945 through February, 1948; and Nathaniel R. Howard, ed., *The Basic Papers of George Humphrey* (Cleveland, 1965), containing speeches, press conferences, congressional testimony, letters and other material of Eisenhower's first Secretary of the Treasury.

The most important memoirs are: Dwight D. Eisenhower, *Mandate for Change, 1953-1956* (Garden City, 1963) and *Waging Peace, 1956-1961* (Garden City, 1965), and Sherman Adams, *Firsthand Report* (New York, 1961). Also important are: Richard M. Nixon, *Six Crises* (Garden City, 1962), especially on Eisenhower's 1955 heart attack; Emmet John Hughes, *The Ordeal of Power* (New York, 1962), on Eisenhower's personality; Lewis L. Strauss, *Men and Decisions* (Garden City, 1962), especially on atomic energy matters; Ezra Taft Benson, *Cross Fire: The Eight Years with Eisenhower* (Garden City, 1962), by the controversial Secretary of Agriculture; Robert Cutler, *No Time For Rest* (Boston, 1966), which is often trivial but has some revealing glimpses of Eisenhower and Secretary of Defense Wilson; E. Frederick Morrow, *Black Man in the White House* (New York, 1963) on subtle or not so subtle racism; and Joseph W. Martin, Jr., *My First Fifty Years in Politics* (New York, 1960), by the House Republican leader.

No genuinely reflective history of the 1950's exists. Two well written stopgaps are Herbert Agar, *The Price of Power: America since 1945* (Chicago, 1957), highly critical of Republicans; and Eric F. Goldman, *The Crucial Decade–and After: America, 1945-1960* (New York, 1961). Hans J. Morgenthau provides a critique in *The Purpose of American Politics* (New York, 1960), especially Parts III and IV. Richard Rovere, *The Eisenhower Years* (New York, 1956) is a collection of skillfully written vignettes and impressions.

There are many biographies of Eisenhower. The best are Herbert S. Parmet, *Eisenhower and the American Crusades* (New York, 1972), Arthur Larson, *Eisenhower: The President Nobody Knows* (New York, 1968), not a formal biography but a friendly analysis; Robert J. Donovan, *Eisenhower: The Inside Story* (New York, 1956); Merlo J. Pusey, *Eisenhower the President* (New York, 1956); Merriman Smith, *Meet Mister Eisenhower* (New York, 1955), all friendly; and Marquis Childs, *Eisenhower: Captive Hero* (New York, 1958), harshly critical.

A group of campaign biographies written for or republished in 1952 are adulatory and reveal "Ike's" image at that time: John Gunther, *Eisenhower: The Man and the Symbol* (New York, 1952); Kenneth S. Davis, *Soldier of Democracy* (New York, 1952), Kevin McCann, *Man from Abilene* (Garden City, 1952), Alden Hatch, *General Ike* (New York, 1944, rev. 1952), and Allan Taylor, *What Eisenhower Thinks* (New York, 1952), portraying the general as moderate, internationalist and conservative.

There are a number of biographies of John Foster Dulles, mostly adulatory or harsh. Louis L. Gerson, *John Foster Dulles* (New York, 1967), in Samuel Flagg Bemis, ed., *The American Secretaries of State and Their Diplomacy* is not very analytical; John R. Beal, *John Foster Dulles* (New York, 1957) is friendly; Eleanor Lansing Dulles, *John Foster Dulles: The Last Year* (New York, 1963), is a sister's memorial; Deane and David Heller, *John Foster Dulles: Soldier for Peace* (New York, 1960) is hagiography. Richard Goold-Adams, *John Foster Dulles: A Reappraisal* (New York, 1962) is a British writer's moderately critical view; Hans J. Morgenthau, "John Foster Dulles" in Norman A. Graebner, ed., *An Uncertain Tradition: American Secretaries of State in the Twentieth Century* (New York, 1961) is savage. More useful are: Andrew H. Berding, *Dulles on Diplomacy* (Princeton, 1965), Dulles' conversations with an Assistant Secretary of State; Michael A. Guhin, "Dulles' Thoughts on International Politics: Myth and Reality," *Orbis*, 13 (Fall, 1969), 865-889; and Guhin's scholarly biography, *John Foster Dulles: A Statesman and His Times* (New York, 1972), portraying the Secretary as neither moralist nor ideologue but as a pragmatist.

Other useful biographies are: Earl Mazo, *Richard Nixon* (New York, 1960); Earl Mazo and Stephen Hess, *Nixon: A Political Portrait* (New York, 1968); Garry Wills, *Nixon Agonistes* (Boston, 1970); William S. White, *The Taft Story* (New York, 1954), friendly to the Senate leader; Joe Alex Morris, *Nelson Rockefeller* (New York, 1960), hostile toward Dulles; William J. Miller, *Henry Cabot Lodge* (New York, 1967) also critical of Dulles, but not of Eisenhower; G. Bernard Noble,

Christian Herter (New York, 1970) in Samuel Flagg Bemis, ed., *The American Secretaries of State and Their Diplomacy.*

On *domestic politics* and Eisenhower as a leader, George H. Mayer, *The Republican Party, 1864-1964* (New York, 1964) is the best survey; Richard M. Scammon, *America at the Polls* (Pittsburgh, 1965) covers the period 1920-1964 through analysis of polls; Samuel Lubell, *Revolt of the Moderates* (New York, 1956) explains the voting trends of the 1950's; Charles A. H. Thomson and Francis M. Shattuck, *The 1956 Presidential Campaign* (Washington, D. C., 1960) is thorough; Arthur Larson, *A Republican Looks at his Party* (New York, 1956) describes and defends the "new Republicanism"; Laurin H. Henry, *Presidential Transitions* (Washington, D. C., 1960) shows Eisenhower shaping an administration in 1952-1953; see Part V. Three older analyses of Presidents are all critical of Eisenhower as a leader: Walter Johnson, *1600 Pennsylvania Avenue: Presidents and the People since 1929* (Boston, 1963), Richard E. Neustadt, *Presidential Power* (New York, 1960); Clinton Rossiter, *The American Presidency* (New York, 1960).

Revisionism began with Murray Kempton, "The Underestimating of Dwight D. Eisenhower," *Esquire*, 68 (September, 1967), 108-9, 156; continues in Garry Wills, *Nixon Agonistes* (Boston, 1970), in "The Hero"; and in Herbert S. Parmet, *Eisenhower* (New York, 1972).

The literature is vast on *American foreign relations* during the 1950's. Good summaries are *The United States in World Affairs*, published annually for the Council on Foreign Relations and edited by various scholars. The best summaries of recent American foreign relations are: Louis J. Halle, *The Cold War as History* (New York, 1967); John W. Spanier, *American Foreign Policy since World War II* (New York, 1971); and Charles O. Lerche, Jr., *The Cold War . . . and After* (Englewood Cliffs, N. J., 1965). Walter LaFeber, *America, Russia and the Cold War* (New York, 1967) tends toward a "New Left" viewpoint. Adam Ulam, *The Rivals: America and Russia since World War II* (New York, 1971) is solid and well written.

Seyom Brown, *The Faces of Power: Constancy and Change in United States Foreign Policy from Truman to Johnson* (New York, 1968) analyzes Dulles' psychology of power as well as Eisenhower's views; W. W. Rostow, *The United States in the World Arena* (New York, 1960) deals with strategic policy; Sidney Warren, *The President as World Leader* (Philadelphia, 1964) is critical of "policy by slogans"; David B. Capitanchik, *The Eisenhower Presidency and American Foreign Policy* (New York, 1969) is critical of Eisenhower as a conservative, passive President; Norman A. Graebner, *The New Isolationism* (New York, 1956) is a contemporary analysis of American attitudes. Robert D. Murphy, *Diplomat Among Warriors* (Garden City, 1964) is the memoir of a noted diplomat.

On the beginnings of U. S. involvement in Vietnam see George McT. Kahin and John W. Lewis, *The United States in Vietnam* (New York, 1971), Edward G. Lansdale, *In the Midst of Wars* (New York, 1972) and Robert Shaplen, *The Lost Revolution* (New York, 1966). On the Suez crisis of 1956 see Hugh Thomas, *Suez* (New

York, 1967) and Kennett Love, *Suez: The Twice-Fought War* (New York, 1969). Herman Finer, *Dulles over Suez* (Chicago, 1964) is sharply critical. Anthony Eden (Lord Avon), *Full Circle* (Boston, 1960) is the British Prime Minister's memoir. See also Harold Macmillan, *Tides of Fortune, 1945-1955* (New York, 1969) and *Riding the Storm, 1956-1959* (New York, 1971). Macmillan worked with Eisenhower during World War II and during the 1950's was British Foreign Secretary, Chancellor of the Exchequer and Prime Minister. On relations with France see John Newhouse, *De Gaulle and the Anglo-Saxons* (New York, 1970) and Charles De Gaulle, *Memoirs of Hope* (New York, 1972).

Maxwell Taylor, *The Uncertain Trumpet* (New York, 1960), by the former chief of staff of the U. S. Army, is critical of "massive retaliation." Taylor's memoirs are *Swords and Plowshares* (New York, 1972).

The question of the "military-industrial complex" has spawned many books. Some are: Richard J. Barnet, *The Economy of Death* (New York, 1972); Fred Cook, *The Warfare State* (New York, 1964); Richard F. Kaufman, *The War Profiteers* (Garden City, 1972); Seymour Melman, *Pentagon Capitalism* (New York, 1970); Clark Mollenhoff, *The Pentagon* (New York, 1967) and George Thayer, *The War Business* (New York, 1969).